Dr AMBEDKAR

The Man Who Shaped India's Democratic Republic

ALSO BY THE SAME AUTHOR

Future of the Indian Education System
How Relevant is the National Education Policy, 2020?

New-Age Technology and Industrial Revolution 4.0
Global Public Policy Issues in Economy, Democracy, National Security and World Peace

Bharat Ratna Dr Babasaheb Ambedkar
An Intellectual Colossus, Great National Leader and Universal Champion of Human Rights (Photo-Biography in English and Marathi)

Ambedkar *An Economist Extraordinaire*

Ambedkar *Awakening India's Social Conscience* (An Intellectual Biography) (English and Marathi)

Ambedkar Writes
Completed Writings of Dr Ambedkar (Edited) (English, Marathi and Hindi)
Vol. I: Political Writings, Vol. II: Scholarly Writings

Ambedkar Speaks
Seminal Speeches Edited: Vol. I, II and III (English 300, Marathi 500)

Trilogy on Ravindranath Tagore (Marathi)
Ravindranath Tagore: Yuga Nirmata Vishvamanav
Ravindranath Tagore: Samagra Sahitya Darshan
Bhaya Shoonya Chitta Jeth: 151 Pratinidhik Kavita

Untouchables
My Family's Triumphant Journey Out of the Caste System in Modern India (International Bestseller – in 15 languages)

Monetary Policy, Financial Stability and Central Banking in India

Re-emerging India – A Global Perspective

Challenges to Indian Banking: Competition, Globalization and Financial Markets (Edited)

Monetary Economics for India

Aamcha Baap Aan Amhi (Marathi, Family Autobiography)
The first international bestseller in Marathi, the book achieved its 200th edition milestone in April 2024. It has sold nearly a million copies in 15 languages, including English, French, Spanish, Korean and Thai.

Dr AMBEDKAR

The Man Who Shaped India's Democratic Republic

Narendra Jadhav

Konark Publishers Pvt. Ltd
206, First Floor,
Peacock Lane, Shahpur Jat,
New Delhi - 110 049
+91-11-4105 5065
india@konarkpublishers.com, us@konarkpublishers.com
www.konarkpublishers.com

ISBN: 978-81-963629-8-0

Edited by Padma Alva

Jacket design by Idesign

Typeset by Saanvi Graphics, Noida

Printed and bound in India by Thomson Press India Ltd.

Dedicated admiringly and affectionately to:
Former Chief Justice of India Shri K.G. Balakrishnan,
Former Chief Justice of India Shri Ranjan Gogoi, and
Current Judge of the Supreme Court of India Justice Bhushan Gavai

Contents

Author's Note

It gives me immense pleasure in introducing this book about the Indian Constitution in the 75th year of India becoming a democratic Republic.

At the end of the World War II, many nations gained independence. But democracy could take roots in very few countries. Indeed, India is a shining example of a thriving functional democracy and that too, in the world's most populous nation. And, the reason behind this is the Indian Constitution.

This book narrates India's journey from 150 years of foreign rule to becoming a sovereign democratic Republic. Central to this long and arduous process was Dr Babasaheb Ambedkar, whose contributions surpassed those of any other Indian leader.

Dr Ambedkar, until recently, was mostly recognised as a Dalit leader, and later, somewhat reluctantly, as the Principal Architect of the Indian Constitution – albeit not unequivocally.

I trust this book demonstrates that Dr Ambedkar not only has the unique distinction of contributing to the process of Constitutional reforms in India throughout but also of drafting and piloting the draft Constitution of India in the high-powered Constituent Assembly, ultimately leading to India becoming a democratic Republic.

That is precisely why Dr Ambedkar should be regarded as *the* person who shaped the Republic of India.

I hope that this book, first of its kind, would be welcomed by scholars, researchers, students, political activists, civil society members and the lay readers alike.

Mumbai **Narendra Jadhav**

Acknowledgements

Editorial Assistance:

Padma Alva, Jiza Joy and Lekshmi Parameswaran

Plagiarism Check:

Kazim Rizvi & Konark Editorial Team

Technical Assistance:

Sruti Kalyanikar and Prabhakar Gaikwad

Other Assistance:

Samir Arora

Family Support:

Vasundhara Jadhav (Wife)
Tanmoy (Son) and Kejal (Daughter-in-law)
Dr Apoorva (Daughter) and Dr Ekim Muyan (Son-in-law)
Agastya, Eymir, Kimaya and Keyan (Grandchildren)

PART I

Dr Ambedkar: Emergence

CHAPTER ONE

Bhim – The Early Days

Dr Bhimrao Ambedkar was born on 14 April 1891 in Mhow (Military Headquarters of War), a small garrison town in Central India (now part of the State of Madhya Pradesh), to an Untouchable family with a history of service in the armed forces. Regionally, the family had its roots in the coastal region of the State of Maharashtra, and in terms of caste, they belonged to the *Mahar* Caste—the largest Untouchable Caste in the State, in terms of population.[1]

Bhimrao's father Ramji as well as his grandfather Maloji had served in the British Army. Ramji enlisted in the military in 1866, eventually attaining the rank of subedar. Later, he served as headmaster of an army school in Mhow. Bhimrao's mother also belonged to a *Mahar* family with a notable military background. She and the women in her family were literate (which was quite unusual for that era) owing to the mandatory education policy for children of army personnel. Ramji and his wife Bhimabai had 14 children, but

1 According to the 1931 Census, *Mahars* constituted nearly 69 per cent of the then Untouchables in the Bombay Presidency compared with 16.2 per cent *Chamars* and 14.9 per cent *Mangs,* the other two major Untouchable Castes.

only five survived. The 14th child, named Bhim (also called Bhiva), was none other than Dr Babasaheb Ambedkar.

With little to no contact with the outside world, Bhim's early childhood in the military cantonment shielded him from the injustices meted out to the Untouchable community. However, this period of protection was short-lived. While Bhim was still a child, the family relocated to Ratnagiri district and later to Satara (both in present-day Maharashtra State), where his father worked as a storekeeper in the Public Works Department.

Early Experiences of Untouchability

In 1900, young Bhim began his schooling at the English medium Government High School in Satara as Bhimrao Ramji Ambavadekar. The surname "Ambavadekar" referred to Ambavade, the family's ancestral village. Bhim's father had changed the surname to shield the family, as the original family surname "Sankpal" gave away their lowly Caste status. Interestingly, one of Bhim's teachers in Satara was a Brahmin named Ambedkar, a phonetic resemblance to Ambavadekar. Bhim, being bright and promising, quickly won the affection of this teacher. To spare Bhim from the long journey home, the kind teacher provided him a daily lunch. In recognition of this kindness, Bhim's family name was later re-registered as Ambedkar, replacing Ambavadekar.

Once Bhim stepped out of the cantonment, devoid of its protective shield against discrimination, he was exposed to the harsh realities of life as an Untouchable. Dr Ambedkar recounted many such experiences in his writings and speeches. These incidents undoubtedly sowed the seeds of rebellion and dissent, which eventually became hallmarks of Dr Ambedkar.

He described a particular incident from his childhood that left a permanent mark on his heart, the pain of which served as a constant reminder of injustice and his responsibility to bring about the much-needed social reforms.

Bhim's father had secured a job as a cashier in Goregaon, located in Satara district. Unable to visit his children during a vacation, he asked them to travel from Satara city to Goregaon. Bhim and his brothers were excited about visiting a new city and undertook a train journey to the nearest railway station called Masur connecting Satara. Upon arrival at Masur, they discovered that contrary to their father's promise, there was no one to receive them at the railway station (they later learned that this miscommunication occurred because their father was unaware of their travel plans for that particular day).

As Dr Ambedkar recalled much later:[2]

> … the Station Master returned and asked as what we proposed to do. We said that if we could get a bullock-cart on hire we would go to Goregaon. … There were many bullock-carts plying for hire. But my reply to the Station Master that we were *Mahars* had gone round among the cartmen, and not one of them was prepared to suffer being polluted and to demean himself carrying passengers of the Untouchable Classes. We were prepared to pay double the fare but we found that money did not work.
>
> The Station Master, who was negotiating on our behalf stood silent not knowing what to do. Suddenly a thought seemed to have entered his head and he asked us, 'Can you drive the cart?' Feeling that he was finding out a solution of our difficulty we shouted, 'yes, we can'. With that answer he went and proposed on our behalf that we were to pay the cart man double the fare and drive the cart and that he should walk on foot along with the cart

2 B. R. Ambedkar, *Waiting for a Visa, Dr Babasaheb Ambedkar Writings and Speeches* (BAWS), Vol. 12, pp. 665-71. BAWS Volumes have been published by the Government of Maharashtra, beginning the year 1979.

on our journey. One cartman agreed as it gave him an opportunity to earn his fare and also saved him from being polluted.

As the brothers started their journey, the situation only deteriorated. Despite packing food, they had not brought sufficient water for the trip. It was during this journey that Bhim discovered the harsh reality: as Untouchables, they were barred from sharing water with the Caste Hindus. Even though they were dressed in fine garments, appearing wealthy, and conversing in the refined language of the privileged, it was not enough to secure water for them during their trip.

Dr Ambedkar recounts these episodes and bares his heart out:[3]

> This incident has a very important place in my life. I was a boy of nine when it happened. But it has left an indelible impression on my mind. Before this incident occurred, I knew that I was an Untouchable and that Untouchables were subjected to certain indignities and discriminations. For instance, I knew that in the school I could not sit in the midst of my class students according to my rank but that I was to sit in a corner by myself. I knew that in the school I was to have a separate piece of gunny cloth for me to squat on in the classroom and the servant employed to clean the school would not touch the gunny cloth used by me and I was required to carry the gunny cloth home in the evening and bring it back the next day.
>
> While in the school I knew that children of the Touchable Classes could go out to the water tap, open it and quench their thirst. I could not touch the tap and unless a Touchable person opened it, I could not quench my thirst. The permission of the teacher was not enough; the presence of the school peon was necessary, for he was the only person whom the class teacher could use for such a purpose. The situation can be summed up in the statement—no peon, no water.

3 Ibid.

At home I know that the working of washing clothes was done by my sisters. Not that there were no washermen in Satara. Not that we could not afford to pay the washermen. Washing was done by my sisters because we were Untouchables and no washerman would wash the clothes of an Untouchable.

The work of cutting the hair or shaving the boys including myself was done by our elder sister who had become quite an expert barber by practicing the art on us, not that there were no barbers in Satara, not that we could not afford to pay the barber. It was because we were Untouchables and no barber would consent to shave an Untouchable.

All this I knew. But this incident gave me a shock such as I never received before, and it made me think about Untouchability, which before this incident happened, was with me as a matter of course, as it is with many Touchables as well as the Untouchables.

Love for Studying

At the tender age of five, Bhim lost his mother in December 1896. When the family relocated to Satara, his father remarried—a situation Bhim found difficult to accept as it meant another woman would replace his mother. He decided to run away to Mumbai (then Bombay) and seek employment in the textile mills. To finance this plan, he decided to steal the required amount from his aunt.

Reflecting on the incident later, Dr Ambedkar recounted, "For three successive nights, I tried to remove the purse tucked at my aunt's waist, but without success. On the fourth night, I did get hold of the purse, but to my disappointment, I found only half an *anna* in it. And in half an *anna*, of course, I could not go to Mumbai."[4]

---

4 As quoted in Dhananjay Keer's *Dr Ambedkar: Life and Mission* (Bombay: Popular Prakashan 1954) p. 75. This biography first appeared when Dr Ambedkar was alive. Accordingly, it is often touted as an official or approved biography of Dr Ambedkar.

This, as fate would have it, proved to be a blessing in disguise and a decisive moment for Bhim. The young boy, once disinterested in studies, underwent a sudden and remarkable transformation overnight! As he later reflected:

> The three nights' experience was so nerve-racking that I gave up the idea of collecting money in this shameful manner and I came to another decision—a decision that gave an entirely different turn to my life. I decided that I must give up my truant habits that I must study hard and get through my examinations as fast as possible, so that I might earn my own livelihood and be independent of my father.[5]

The result? The little boy, who once harboured aspirations of becoming a mill worker in Mumbai, grew up to achieve the feat of being the Labour Minister of India in the Viceroy's Executive Council (1942-46).

It was Bhim's father who played a significant role in his early education. A follower of the Kabir *Panth*, Ramji frequently hosted devotional singing sessions (*Bhajans*) and recitation of holy texts at their home. Influenced by Jyotiba Phule, the force behind major social reforms among non-Brahmins in the later 19th century, Ramji instilled similar values in his son. It comes as no surprise that years later, Dr Ambedkar regarded Buddha, Kabir and Phule as his three *Gurus*.

Ramji also instilled in Bhim a deep love for books. He aspired for his son to pursue studies not just for the sake of passing examinations, but also to excel with flying colours.

In 1904, Ramji was laid off and decided to move to Mumbai along with his family. Bhim enrolled at Elphinstone High School to continue his education. Ramji encouraged him and even used his

---

5 *Ibid*, p.76.

pension to buy almost any book that Bhim desired. Despite financial constraints, Ramji ensured that Bhim's curiosity for knowledge was never hindered. Even when funds ran low, Ramji would persuade his sister to part with her jewellery, which he would pawn to buy more books until the next instalment of his pension arrived. Sacrifices were inevitable due to their meagre income, making it impossible for the family to afford the education of both sons. So, the elder son, Balaram, took up employment in a factory while Bhim continued his studies at Elphinstone High School.

During his time at school, Bhim faced the harsh realities of caste discrimination. He was once summoned by a teacher to solve an arithmetic problem on the blackboard in front of the whole classroom. Chaos ensued as the Caste Hindu children rushed to remove their lunch boxes placed near the blackboard, fearing "pollution". When Bhim expressed a desire to study Sanskrit, he was told that Untouchables were prohibited from studying the sacred language of the *Vedas* and could only opt for either English or Persian. These reminders of Untouchability undoubtedly left lasting scars on the impressionable Bhim.

As a young boy, Bhim was not particularly popular among his peers and was often involved in fights with schoolmates. He spent much of his time engrossed in a book in a nearby garden, where he caught the eye of social activist Krishnaji Arjun Keluskar, the Principal of Wilson High School at the time. Keluskar took the diligent and studious boy under his wing, becoming a significant well-wisher and supporter for years to come.

While still a high school student, Bhim, at the age of 14, married Ramabai, a nine-year-old girl, in 1905. It was an arranged marriage.[6] The venue for the marriage ceremony was also rather unusual. It

---

6 While this is shocking for contemporary sensibilities, it was quite normal in the early 20th century India.

took place at the open market shed of the Byculla Vegetable Market in Mumbai after business hours.

Seven years later, Bhim became a father when Yashwant was born, and although four more children followed, only Yashwant survived.

In 1907, Bhim passed his Matriculation examination from Elphinstone High School. This was an unheard of feat for an Untouchable and called for celebrations in his community. After the public ceremony, Principal Keluskar presented Bhim with a biography of the Buddha titled *Life of Gautam Buddha.* Little did either of them imagine that in the years to come, Dr Ambedkar would emerge as a great champion of Buddhism and would be instrumental in transforming the lives of millions of Untouchables by guiding them onto the path of Buddha.

Having completed his initial schooling, Bhimrao was encouraged by his father to pursue further studies at Elphinstone College in Mumbai. However, even there, Bhimrao encountered instances of Untouchability, such as when the Brahmin canteen owner at the college refused to give him tea or water. Fortunately, once again, some teachers showed kindness and lent him a helping hand. One such teacher was a European named Professor Muller, who lent Bhimrao books and gave him clothes.

Bhimrao began his studies with full vigour, but due to ill-health, he had to take a year off. When Bhimrao passed his Intermediate examination, his father could not afford his fees, prompting Principal Keluskar to step forward. Keluskar arranged a scholarship for Bhimrao from the Princely State of Baroda. With this immense support and belief in his potential, Bhimrao joined Elphinstone College on a scholarship of Rs 25 per month.

Bhimrao resumed his college education and started working very hard. Around that time, the family moved their residence to Parel – Bombay Improvement Trust (BIT) *Chawl* Number 1. Dr Ambedkar mentioned many years later that in those two rooms lived a family of 10 (parents, brothers and sisters' children) and one she-goat. He devoted himself to his studies, sometimes studying up to 21 hours a day by the dim glow of a kerosene lamp.[7] In 1912, he earned his BA degree in Economics and Political Science from Bombay University. It was in this fashion—overcoming not only health setbacks but also social injustices and financial hardships—that Bhimrao became one of the first Untouchables in India to become a graduate.

As a college graduate at the age of 22, Bhimrao got employed as a Probationer in the Accountant General Office of the State of Baroda, with a monthly salary of Rs 75 as per the Scholarship Agreement. His father, however, expressed dismay at this decision, fearing that the traditional and casteist society of the erstwhile Baroda State (as perceived by him) would continue to subject Bhimrao to the restrictions of Untouchability, something that was not as prevalent in the liberal and cosmopolitan environment of Mumbai.

On reaching Baroda, Ramji's fears were proven right. Bhimrao struggled to find suitable accommodation and had to take shelter in the sleeping quarters at the Arya Samaj office. Moreover, he was forced to dine in a distant Untouchable neighbourhood due to caste discrimination. His professional prospects were equally bleak, as he was tossed across departments and deprived of any meaningful work. Still, he persisted for another 15 days. However, news of his father's illness compelled him to return to Mumbai, where his father passed away on 2 February 1913.

Thanks to the generosity of Principal Keluskar, Bhimrao later had the opportunity to present his case before the Maharaja of Baroda

---

7 Marathi Speech at the Pune Untouchables Students' Conference, Pune (11 September 1928). For the complete text of the speech, refer to *Ambedkar Speaks,* which features thematically edited 300 speeches in English and 500 speeches in Marathi across three volumes (Narendra Jadhav (ed.), Vol. I, 2013, pp. 443-48).

in Mumbai. The kind-hearted Maharaja, Sayajirao Gaikwad, offered a scholarship (£11.50 a month for two years) for Bhimrao to study at Columbia University in New York. In return, Bhimrao committed to serving the State of Baroda for 10 years upon completion of his education abroad.

This was an unprecedented opportunity for young Bhimrao, and indeed, for any Untouchable, at that time.

CHAPTER TWO

The Advent of Dr Ambedkar

The chance to go to the US for higher studies marked the first significant turning point in the life of young Bhimrao Ambedkar. It had the potential to profoundly reshape the trajectory and destiny of the bright and diligent Untouchable Bhimrao, altering his path forever.

MA and PhD at Columbia University, USA

In 1913, a new and exciting chapter unfolded in the life of Bhimrao as he embarked upon his Postgraduate Studies at Columbia University in New York. He was among the first group of Indians to pursue advanced training in economics in the early 20th century in the US. However, unlike his peers, Bhimrao's journey was daunting with constant tussles against the dual challenges of poverty and Caste-based discrimination.

At Columbia University, Bhimrao had the privilege of learning from several great thinkers such as philosopher John Dewey, anthropologist A.A. Goldenweiser and economist Edwin Seligman, all of whom were his teachers at the University. In 1915, under the support and guidance of Professor Seligman, a leading authority in Public Finance and History of Economic Thought, Bhimrao successfully finished his MA. He was merely 24. His Master's thesis focused on the 'Administration and Finance of the East India Company'.

In a span of just two years, by the time he reached the age of 26, Bhimrao had submitted his PhD Dissertation, which was approved, granting him a Doctorate in 1917. His PhD Dissertation was titled 'National Dividend: A Historical and Analytical Study'. Years later, in 1925, his Dissertation was published as a book titled *The Evolution of Provincial Finance in British India,* and he was formally awarded his PhD degree by Columbia University (June 1927).[1]

Thoughtfully, Dr Ambedkar dedicated the book to the then Maharaja of Baroda Shri Sayajirao Gaikwad, "*as a token of gratitude for his help in the matter of my education*".

Professor Edwin Seligman, his teacher at Columbia University, from whom Dr Ambedkar learnt his "first lessons in the theory of Public Finance", said in his foreword: "The value of Mr Ambedkar's contribution ... lies in the objective recitation of the facts and the impartial analysis of the interesting development that has taken place in his native country. The lessons are applicable to the other countries as well; nowhere to my knowledge has such a detailed study of the underlying principles been made."

This book represents Dr Ambedkar's pioneering contribution to the field of Public Finance. In this book, he deals with the Centre-State financial relationship in British India during the period 1833 to 1921. He presents a pioneering study of the origin, development and mechanism of Provincial finance in India. The analytical insights provided by him in the Centre-Provincial financial relationship are

---

1 According to the then prevailing University rules, students were required to publish their dissertations in book form and submit copies to the University to formally receive their PhD degree.

as relevant today as they were when this pioneering work was first brought out.

* * *

During his doctoral studies at Columbia University, Dr Ambedkar also took an Anthropology Seminar under Prof. Goldenweiser. As a participant in the Seminar, Dr Ambedkar presented a Research Paper to the fellow-students titled 'Castes in India, Their Mechanism, Genesis and Development', on 9 May 1916.[2]

Dr Ambedkar was only 25 when he wrote this brilliant research paper. As noted, "still in his mid-twenties, the prodigious Ambedkar writes of being troubled by the ghost of Manu, that mystical jurist of Hindu tradition, whose classic work *Manusmriti* he will publicly burn in 1927."[3]

DSc and Bar-at-Law in Britain

Having completed his MA and PhD from the US, Dr Ambedkar was determined to obtain another Doctorate from the London School of Economics and also to qualify as a Barrister. This was essential for him to establish a career in law while simultaneously devoting time to social work and writing books, once he fulfilled the terms of his scholarship agreement of serving the State of Baroda.

However, an obstacle arose. His scholarship support was scheduled to end in June 1916. In order to achieve his goals, he needed a two-year extension to the scholarship. His request for

2 The paper was published in *India Antiquary*, May 1917. For full summary, see *Ambedkar Writes* (ed. Narendra Jadhav, 2014) – thematically edited all completed works in English and Marathi in two volumes, Vol. II, Scholarly Writings, pp. 19-36.

3 Aishwary Kumar, 'The Lies of Manu', *Outlook*, 20 August 2012. https://magazine.outlookindia.com/story/the-lies-of-manu/281937

extension was denied. Feeling dejected and desperate, Dr Ambedkar followed the advice of his PhD guide Prof. Seligman, and re-applied for an extension with a strong letter of recommendation from Prof. Seligman. Eventually, the Maharaja of Baroda intervened, but the extension was only for one year.

Undeterred, the "indomitable" Dr Ambedkar hit the ground running for London in May 1916, even before receiving approval for the extension of his scholarship. Carrying a letter of recommendation from Prof. Seligman to Prof. Sydney Webb, a great economist and thinker at the London School of Economics, Dr Ambedkar embarked on this journey with no money in his pocket.

Upon reaching Liverpool by ship, Dr Ambedkar underwent thorough scrutiny by British authorities due to suspicions that he may have ties with the Indian Revolutionary Army. After great efforts, he was cleared for release following the verification of his recommendation letters. Risking the journey to London without a ticket, Dr Ambedkar reached his destination without being caught. Fortunately, two days later, a letter from the Government of Baroda—awarding Dr Ambedkar a one-year extension for his scholarship—arrived.

Dr Ambedkar was admitted to the London School of Economics and Political Science on 11 October 1916 and to the Grey's Inn for Bar-at-Law on 11 November 1916. With his admission secured, he dedicated himself to his studies with full vigour. A few months later, he reapplied to the Maharaja of Baroda to grant another extension. Unfortunately, his request was not only firmly declined, but he was also instructed to return to India to fulfil his commitment to serve the Baroda Government and honour the Scholarship Agreement.

Left with no alternative, Dr Ambedkar had to comply and return to India. Backed against the wall, he reached out to the London School of Economics, seeking leniency for the unexpected interruption in his studies and requesting additional time. The

University of London "excused the interruption of his course of study for a period not exceeding four years from October 1917". Similar leave was also granted from Grey's Inn.

* * *

On Dr Ambedkar's arrival in Mumbai, a felicitation function was organized in Mumbai under the Chairmanship of the then Chief Presidency Magistrate of Bombay. Depressed and dejected, Dr Ambedkar did not attend the function.

Under the terms of the Scholarship Agreement with the Baroda State, Bhimrao had committed to serving the Princely State for 10 years in exchange for the financial support provided for his education abroad. Initially, the Maharaja expressed a desire to appoint Dr Ambedkar as the Finance Minister of the Baroda State. However, upon his return to Baroda in 1917, Bhimrao was appointed as the Maharaja's Military Secretary, with a monthly remuneration of Rs 150.

Despite attaining exceptionally strong academic credentials, Dr Ambedkar remained vulnerable to the pervasive influence of the Caste-ridden system. Even with his advanced degrees and high-ranking position in the service, he could not evade the stigma of Untouchability. Due to his Caste, he struggled to find housing in Baroda and ultimately had to adopt a Parsi name to secure accommodation in a Parsi Boarding Home.

His workplace provided no respite either. Brahmin clerks and subordinates were regularly insubordinate, maintaining physical distance by literally tossing papers and files onto his desk to avoid contact.[4] When he attempted to join a club frequented by officers, he found himself seated at a corner and unwelcome to participate in any activities. Confronted with a hostile and conservative atmosphere in

---

4 This was "social distancing" at its worst.

Baroda, Dr Ambedkar struggled to make friends and was compelled to seek solace in solitude.

The dehumanising treatment reached a critical point when an enraged mob of Parsis besieged the Boarding House where Dr Ambedkar resided, determined to physically assault him. This fiasco was later described by Dr Ambedkar himself as follows:[5]

> This scene of a dozen Parsis armed with sticks lined [up] before me in a menacing mood, and myself standing before them with a terrified look imploring for mercy, is a scene which so long a period as eighteen years has not succeeded in fading away. I can even now vividly recall it - and [I] never recall it without tears in my eyes. It was then for the first time that I learnt that a person who is an Untouchable to a Hindu is also an Untouchable to a Parsi.

Feeling utterly dejected, humiliated and helpless, Dr Ambedkar submitted his resignation and returned to Mumbai on 31 August 1917.

Upon reaching Mumbai, Dr Ambedkar tried to making a living for his growing family. However, tragedy struck when his elder brother Anandrao, who had been providing for the family, passed away in November 1917, leaving Dr Ambedkar in dire straits. Despite his efforts, he struggled to make ends meet. He worked as a private tutor and accountant for a Parsi businessman, earning Rs 50 per month. He also established a small firm for stockbroking and worked as an investment consultant. However, his clients rejected him upon discovering his Caste status.

With few options remaining, Dr Ambedkar began teaching Economics, Banking and Mercantile Law at Davar's College of Commerce for a meagre remuneration of Rs 50 per month. With a

---

5 Ambedkar, *Waiting for a Visa,* pp. 676-78.

total monthly income of Rs 150, it was barely possible to scrape a living. Saving for his incomplete education abroad seemed nearly impossible. As Blake Clarke aptly noted later,[6] "one of India's best educated man lived in Bombay for the next year and half, unemployed, poverty-stricken and miserable."

After enduring a lot of struggles and frustrating endeavours, Dr Ambedkar secured a one-year position as Professor of Political Economy at Sydenham College, Mumbai, with a monthly salary of Rs 450. He held this position from 11 November 1918 to 11 March 1920. Even in this role, his popularity with the students sharply contrasted with the Untouchability he experienced from fellow teachers.

In 1920, Dr Ambedkar began an important initiative—the publication of a fortnightly titled *Mook Nayak* (the Leader of the Silent) in Mumbai. This time, he received support from a visionary ruler Maharaja Shahu Chhatrapati of Kolhapur. While Dr Ambedkar could not serve as the editor of *Mook Nayak* due to his position as Professor in a Government College, the fortnightly became his mouthpiece. Through this publication, he criticised the Indian political community for their unwillingness to fight Caste-based discrimination.

In the first issue of *Mook Nayak* on 31 January 1920, Dr Ambedkar advocated for the establishment of a platform "to deliberate on the injustices let loose or likely to be imposed on us and other Depressed people and to think of their future development and appropriate strategies towards it critically". Comparing Hindu Society to a tower with several storeys but lacking a ladder or an entrance, he asserted that one must die in the storey in which one was born. He argued that herculean efforts were necessary to uplift the Depressed Classes

---

6 Blake Clarke, 'Ambedkar: The Untouchable', *Christian Herald*, March 1950, p. 80.

from perpetual slavery, poverty and ignorance, emphasising the need to awaken them to their predicament.

Dr Ambedkar started for London on 5 July 1920 to resume his advanced studies, with the support from Maharaja Shahu of Kolhapur Princely State, a personal loan of Rs 5,000 from an old Parsi friend, Naval Bhathena, and his own savings of Rs 7,000.

* * *

After arriving back in London in August 1920, Dr Ambedkar resumed his studies in September of the same year, both at the London School of Economics and Political Science, as well as for the Bar at the Grey's Inn.

Given the small sum of money available to him, life was one of extreme abstinence and hardship for the young scholar. Residing at a boarding house, he would start his day at 6 a.m. After quickly consuming a piece of bread with a bit of jam and a serving of fish along with a cup of tea, he would be the first to arrive at the library, and immerse in intense reading. So engrossed was he in taking copious notes that he often skipped lunch. A diligent student, he would always be the last person to leave the library, and that too only after a friendly reminder by the security guards. After a short walk and an early dinner, he would resume his studies until the early hours of dawn. Even his Indian roommate pleaded with him to rest, but the unstoppable Dr Ambedkar only responded, "No money, no food; no time, no sleep!"

Soon, Dr Ambedkar's relentless research bore fruit, earning him a Master of Science (MSc) degree in June 1921 for his Thesis, 'Provincial Decentralization of Imperial Finance in British India'. In early 1922, he submitted his Dissertation titled 'The Problem of the Rupee' for his DSc degree, guided by another eminent economist Professor Edwin Cannon. On 28 June 1922, Dr Ambedkar was invited to the Bar i.e., to become a Barrister.

Meanwhile, Dr Ambedkar decided to pursue further studies in Germany. While awaiting clearance from Bonn University, he commenced studying both German and French. Upon receiving the necessary approvals, he left for Germany. However, he soon learned that his Doctoral Dissertation had been rejected by his London examiners. He decided to rewrite it, but maintained the conclusions outlined in the original thesis.

In April 1923, Dr Ambedkar returned to Mumbai due to financial constraints. Seizing this opportunity, he revised his Dissertation and forwarded it to London within five months. In November 1923, he received a telegram informing him that he had been awarded the degree of Doctor of Science (DSc) in Economics, and his Dissertation titled *The Problem of the Rupee: Its Origin and Its Solution* was published as a book.

This Dissertation made a significant contribution to the field of Monetary Economics. The book was aptly dedicated to the memory of his parents, as a token of his lifelong gratitude for their selfless sacrifices and their commitment to his education.

Prof. Edwin Cannon, his Guide, who wrote the Foreword to his book, said:

> I disagree with the good deal of his criticism ... I do not share Dr Ambedkar's hostility to the system, nor accept most of his arguments against it and its advocates. But he hits some nails very squarely on the head, and even when I have thought him quite wrong, I have found a stimulating freshness in his views and reasons ... In his practical conclusion, I am inclined to think, he is right.

The Problem of the Rupee is truly a magnum opus. In this book, Dr Ambedkar offers an excellent exposition of the evolution of the Indian currency in terms of its form as a medium of exchange and its equivalence in terms of precious metals, such as gold and silver.

Unlike the treatises then available, Dr Ambedkar goes into the most neglected period extending from 1800 to 1893. With this historical perspective brought up to the early 1920s, Dr Ambedkar then focuses on one of the most perplexing problem at that time, viz., the choice of an appropriate currency system for India. It was in respect of the currency crisis of the 1920s that Dr Ambedkar crossed swords with influential economic thinkers like John Maynard Keynes, etc.

Dr Ambedkar vehemently criticized Keynes and other supporters of the Gold Exchange Standard and argued in favour of the Gold Standard in a modified form. Dr Ambedkar proposed that all further coinage of the Rupee should be permanently prohibited; a suitable gold coin be minted; the ratio between the gold coin and the Rupee may be fixed by law and the Rupee and the gold coin should not be mutually convertible. In course of time, India would thus have Rupee as well as gold coins as unlimited legal tender, since the ratio between the gold coin and the rupee is fixed under the law and the supply of gold is stable. He further argued that issue of currency would be regulated leading to stable prices and hence a stable currency standard.

Dr Ambedkar had now become a Barrister with two Doctoral Degrees in Economics—a PhD from Columbia University, USA, and a DSc from London School of Economics. He had accomplished an extraordinary feat, something that was exceedingly challenging for anybody, and simply phenomenal for an Untouchable!

CHAPTER THREE

Assimilating the Liberal Republicanism[1]

The beginning of the 20th century saw England emerging as the preferred destination for Indian students seeking higher education. England was renowned for its prestigious academic institutions that were centuries old. However, for young Bhimrao, the chance to study in the US presented a distinct opportunity. Unlike England's colonial institutions, America stood as a thriving democracy. The values of liberty, equality and fraternity were enshrined in the American Constitution.

Life in the US provided Bhimrao with a glimpse of a "free world". For the first time, he grasped and appreciated the true essence of freedom. He had the freedom to move according to his own will

---

1 Liberalism is seen here as a political and moral philosophy grounded in individual liberty and equality under the law. On the other hand, Republicanism is viewed as a political ideology centred on citizenship in a State organized as a Republic. The essence of classical Republicanism lies in uncompromising commitment to liberty (and a total rejection of aristocracy) and in abiding faith in "unalienable" or natural rights of individuals.

and to interact with others as equals—an entirely new experience for him. He woke up each day with a new purpose and meaning. This ignited an unquenchable quest for knowledge within him, a characteristic that defined him for the rest of his life.

It was in America that Bhimrao also realized the importance of education—for both male and female—as the only panacea for the upliftment of the Untouchables. Interestingly, in a letter to a family friend in the very first month of his stay at the Columbia University, he said, quoting Shakespeare: "*There is a tide in the affairs of men. Which, taken at the flood, leads on to fortune; Omitted, all the voyage of their life is bound in shallows and miseries…*"

Bhimrao wrote that "our (i.e., that of Untouchables) progress will be greatly accelerated if male education is pursued side by side with female education…"

Bhimrao, a young man of 22, advised his elderly family friend: "Let your mission, therefore, be to educate and preach the idea of education to those at least who are near to, and in close contact with you."[2]

Before going to the US, young Bhimrao had believed that spreading education among the Depressed Classes would be enough to qualify them for Government jobs. His American education changed all that. His mental horizons widened, and his global view was completely transformed.

Bhimrao realized that mere spread of education and (even) getting Government jobs for Untouchables would never solve the main problem of social disabilities. It became evident to him that the Untouchables would have to be made conscious about their social and political rights. For this purpose, they needed to be imbued with

---

2 C.B. Khairmode, *Dr Bhimrao Ramji Ambedkar,* Vol. I-XII [Marathi] (Pune: Sugava Prakashan, 1984-2008).

new dynamism through mass awakening. Indeed, this became the young Bhimrao's mission in life, while still studying in the US.[3]

* * *

Young Bhimrao Ambedkar's arrival in the US in 1913 coincided with a period when the American society itself was going through a major upheaval and reformation. Fifty years ago, President Abraham Lincoln enacted the Emancipation Proclamation in 1863, declaring "that all persons held as slaves" within the rebellious states "are, and hence forward shall be free". This Declaration led to three supportive amendments to the US Constitution, collectively known as the Reformation Amendments (1865, 1868 and 1870).

Unfortunately, within seven years thereafter, discrimination against African Americans resurfaced (1877) through the implementation of 'Black Codes' (which restricted African Americans to menial labour occupations) and 'Jim Crow Laws' (resulting in the ghettoization of African Americans and restriction of their access to public utilities).

When Bhimrao arrived in the US in the second decade of the 20th century, he witnessed the country's movements against racial and gender inequalities. The African American community's efforts were helmed by Booker T. Washington (1856-1918) and William Du Bois (1868-1963), each advocating for equality in distinct ways. During Ambedkar's stay in the US, Booker T. Washington's influence was waning, while William Du Bois was gaining prominence. In fact, when Bhimrao arrived in New York, the National Association for Advancement of the Coloured People (NAACP), the largest and most pre-eminent civil rights organization in the US, was in its nascent stages, having been founded just a few years ago earlier with Du Bois

3 Ibid.

as a co-founder. By then, Du Bois had become the most prominent voice of reason against the 'Black Codes' and 'Jim Crow Laws'.

Simultaneously, the US was also gripped with the emergence of another historic movement: the Women's Suffrage Movement. In this context, two major events marked the year 1913 of Bhimrao's arrival in the US. First, Alice Paul (one of the foremost leaders of the campaign which brought about an amendment to the US Constitution prohibiting sex discrimination in the right to vote) spearheaded the Woman's Suffrage Procession in Washington D.C., the largest one till then. The parade was attacked, but no arrests were made. Secondly, the US Senate voted on a Women's Suffrage amendment for giving women the right to vote, however it failed to become an Act.[4]

Young Bhimrao must have followed these developments and the fight for equality ardently and with keen interest. But there is no record of him participating in this revolution or his thoughts on it, or his experience of living in the close proximity of Harlem[5] which is just a stone's throw away from Columbia University, wherein he was enrolled.

Later when Dr Bhimrao was studying in London, Lala Lajpat Rai—who played a pivotal role in India's Freedom Struggle—attempted to bring him to "join the political, if not the revolutionary movement, for the freedom of India". Apparently, Dr Bhimrao "told the great leader of India that he was a student and he must complete his studies without betraying the sacred trust of the Maharaja who had given him an opportunity in his life".[6]

---

4 It took seven more years for women in the US to finally get the right to vote, when the Nineteenth Amendment to the US Constitution was ratified in 1920.

5 Harlem is traditionally known as the "Black Mecca of the world".

6 Keer, *Dr Ambedkar*(Third Edition, Reprint 2005), p 27.

Undoubtedly, young Bhimrao had to prioritize his studies. The same deliberation might have been the reason for Bhimrao being not an active participant in the social movements of the US at that time, in spite of the fact that they were so close to his heart, as time would tell.

* * *

During his time at Columbia University, Bhimrao chose to study Moral Philosophy, Anthropology, Sociology and Economics. Over the period of three years (including summers) he took up 29 course credits in Economics, 11 in History, six in Sociology, five in Philosophy, four in Anthropology, three in Politics, and one each in Elementary French and German. All this hard work was going to come in handy when the young Bhimrao would eventually lead the Untouchables of India towards the path of equality, self-dignity and empowerment.

Dr Ambedkar, Prof. Dewey and Thomas Paine

At Columbia University, he had special affinity towards Prof. John Dewey. Prof. Dewey was the one "whom I owe so much", he fondly reminisced much later. Mr Dewey (1859–1952) was a Professor of Philosophy at Columbia University. Bhimrao was impressed by Prof. Dewey's liberal and humanistic approach in his "Philosophy of Pragmatism".

Prof. Dewey, as a social and political philosopher, worked on societal problems like poor sanitation, inhuman working conditions, income inequality and the exclusion of some strata of the society. Prof. Dewey's "Philosophy of Pragmatism" stepped away from abstractions such as: "Being", "Essence" and "Truth".[7] Prof. Dewey's

7 Lane W. Lancaster, *Masters of Political Thought: Hegel To Dewey*, Vol. III (London: George G. Harrap and Co Ltd, 1975), p. 332.

philosophy focused on providing social status and dignity to everyone in society across professions, dignified and menial alike. This refreshing perspective is precisely what must have greatly interested young Bhimrao.

Bhimrao's favourite quotation of Prof. Dewey was: "Every society gets encumbered with what is trivial, with deadwood from the past and with what is positively perverse.... As a society becomes more enlightened, it realizes that it is responsible not to conserve and transmit the whole of its existing achievements, but only such as make for a better future society."

Dr Ambedkar referenced him in his epochal essay 'Annihilation of Caste' (1936) to criticise orthodox Hindus fixated on reviving India's so-called glorious past. He advocated for the moral and intellectual regeneration of Hindu society, emphasizing that preoccupation with past glory hindered such progress.

Young Bhimrao was influenced by another great American Philosopher and Political Theorist Thomas Paine (1737–1809). Prof. Jagdish Shivpuri[8] told me on several occasions that Dr Ambedkar often spoke of Thomas Paine's book *Rights of Man* (first published in 1791), and never tired of quoting from it. Some of his favourites were:

- "The world is my country, all mankind are my brethren, and to do good is my religion."
- "Man did not enter into society to become worse than he was before, nor to have fewer rights than he had before, but to have those rights better secured."

8 Prof. Shivpuri was a colleague of Dr Ambedkar and taught English at Siddharth College, founded by Dr Ambedkar. Prof. Shivpuri was personally recruited by Dr Ambedkar.

- "Whatever is my right as a man is also the right of another; and it becomes my duty to guarantee as well as possess."

The egalitarian individualism of Thomas Paine left a lasting impression on him. They shaped the liberal and republican mindset of young Bhimrao.

* * *

During his time in New York at Columbia University, as well as in London, and later upon returning to India, Dr Ambedkar read the works of a broad spectrum of Western thinkers, philosophers and historians who wrote about the welfare of humanity. These included ancient Greek philosophers such as Socrates (470 BC–399 BC), Thucydides (460 BC–400 BC), Thrasymachus (459 BC–400 BC), Plato (424 BC–347 BC) and Aristotle (384 BC–322 BC), as well as later European scholars such as Prof. Martin Luther (1483–1546), Voltaire (1694–1778), Edmund Burke (1729–1797), Daniel O'Connell (1775–1847), John Stuart Mill (1806–1873), Bertrand Russel (1872–1970) and Harold Laski (1893–1950).

On the other side of the Atlantic, besides Prof. John Dewey and Thomas Paine, Dr Ambedkar closely studied American scholars such as Thomas Jefferson (1743–1826), William Garrison (1805–1879), Fredrick Douglass (1818–1895), Abraham Lincoln (1809–1865), Booker T. Washington (1856–1918) and William Du Bois (1868–1963).

All these great scholars left a mark on young Bhimrao's mind. In fact, Dr Ambedkar referenced many of these philosophers and historians in a lot of his speeches[9] as well as in his prolific scholarly writings.[10]

---

9 Jadhav, *Ambedkar Speaks*

10 Jadhav, *Ambedkar Writes*

Indeed, it is possible to get insights into the intellectual impact of these scholars on Dr Ambedkar by analysing their quotes used by him. An interesting attempt in that direction has already been made.[11]

Dr Ambedkar, Lincoln, Booker T. Washington and William Du Bois

Dr Ambedkar's "approved" biographer, Dhananjay Keer has claimed:[12] "While in America, Ambedkar's mind must have been deeply impressed with two things ... 'the fourteenth Amendment to that {i.e. US} Constitution which declares the freedom of Negroes. The second was the life of Booker T Washington ...' whose work '... broke the shackles of bondage which had crushed the Negroes for ages physically, mentally and spiritually'."

However, these claims do not find proof as discussed below.

Given his lived experience of the social inequalities faced by Untouchables, it is undeniable that the racial problems in the US were very close to Dr Ambedkar's heart and he analysed them thoroughly.

Dr Ambedkar, in fact, drew parallels between the two inhuman institutions—Slavery and Caste System—and called Untouchables in India "the children of India's ghetto".[13] He said:

---

11 D.T. Khabde, 'The influence of western liberal thinkers on the thoughts of Dr B.R. Ambedkar' (PhD Dissertation submitted to Dr Babasaheb Ambedkar Marathwada University [BAMU] in 1985). This chapter, to an extent, draws from this Dissertation, available at https://shodhganga.inflibnet.ac.in/bitstream/10603/102948/1/01_title%20page.pdf.

12 Keer, *Dr Ambedkar,* p. 31.

13 Dr Ambedkar, 'Untouchables or the Children of India's Ghetto' (unpublished manuscript published by the Government of Maharashtra after Dr Ambedkar's death). See BAWS, Vol. V, p. 15.

> Slavery was never obligatory. But Untouchability is obligatory. The law of slavery permitted emancipation. Once a slave always a slave was *not* the fate of the slave. In Untouchability there is no escape. Once an Untouchable, always an Untouchable. The other difference is that Untouchability is an indirect form of slavery. A deprivation of a man's freedom by an open and direct way is preferable form of enslavement. It makes the slave conscious of his enslavement and to become conscious of slavery is the first and most important step in the battle for freedom. But if a man deprived of his liberty indirectly, he has no consciousness of his enslavement. Untouchability is an indirect form of slavery.

The American Declaration of Independence of 1776 left a mark on Dr Ambedkar, with Thomas Jefferson stating that: "We hold these truths to be self-evident, that all men are created equal; that they are endowed by their Creator with certain unalienable Rights; that among these are Life, Liberty and the pursuit of Happiness. That to secure these rights, Governments are instituted among Men, deriving their just powers from the consent of the governed."[14]

Dr Ambedkar, however, notes that "The implementation of this Declaration has no doubt been a tragic episode in the history of the United States ... this charter of human Liberty was not applied to the Negroes. ... There is no doubt ... about the faith of Jefferson ... . He wrote, 'I am sorry for my countrymen'."

Another important person whose work greatly influenced Dr Ambedkar was William Lloyd Garrison, a white social reformer and journalist who founded anti-slavery newspaper called *The Liberator* in 1831. Dr Ambedkar recited him in many of his speeches and

14 B.R. Ambedkar, *Mr Gandhi and the Emancipation of the Untouchables*, Monograph, first published in 1943. BAWS Vol. IX. For summary, see Jadhav, *Ambedkar Writes,*Vol. I, p. 256. Both quotes are from the same source.

writings directly or indirectly. What Garrison wrote in the first issue of *The Liberator* was close to Dr Ambedkar's heart:[15]

> I shall strenuously contend for the immediate enforcement of our slave population .... On this subject, I do not wish to write, or speak or think, with moderation. No. No. Tell a man whose house is on fire, to give a moderate alarm. Tell him to moderately rescue his wife from the hands of the ravisher. Tell the mother to gradually extricate her babe from the fire into which she has fallen, but urge me not into moderation in a cause like the present. I am in earnest – I will not excuse – I will not retreat a single inch and I will be heard.[16]

* * *

When President Abraham Lincoln signed the Emancipation Proclamation (1 January 1863), it undeniably laid the foundation for the abolition of slavery in the US. Dr Ambedkar who read extensively about the life and work of Abraham Lincoln was certainly moved by his sincerity in wanting liberation for the slaves. Dr Ambedkar also admired President Lincoln's appeal during the American Civil War that the nation shall not survive half slave and half free.

Notably, Dr Ambedkar had however, reached a conclusion that Lincoln's Emancipation Proclamation was a matter of political expediency. "In the case of both, Mr Gandhi and Lincoln, the emancipation of the suppressed people was a matter of political expediency."[17]

Dr Ambedkar's view of Lincoln's policy seems to have been shaped by Bertrand Russell's book, *Freedom versus Organization, 1814-1914*, first published in 1934, where he quotes from Lincoln's

15 Khabde, PhD Dissertation.

16 Ibid.

17 Ibid.

letter to a friend saying "my paramount object in this struggle is to save the Union and not either to save or destroy slavery. It was only a military measure …".[18]

One of the earliest African American social reformers Frederick Douglass must have left a mark on Dr Ambedkar. Douglass, who was a great orator, said in a speech in New York (3 August 1857) – i.e., about five years *before* the Emancipation Proclamation, that: "… If there is no struggle there is no progress. Those who profess to favour freedom and yet deprecate agitation are men who want crops without ploughing up the ground … The limits of tyrants are prescribed by the endurance of those who they oppress."[19]

Dr Ambedkar was well aware that after the Emancipation Declaration of 1863, there was a brief period of "Reconstruction". During this time, three important changes were brought about in the US Constitution:

13th Amendment:	Former slaves ceased to be slaves (1865);
14th Amendment:	Former slaves given citizenship rights and equal protection under law (1868); and
15th Amendment:	Right to vote given irrespective of "race, colour or previous condition of servitude" (1870).

All three 'Reconstruction' Amendments were commendable indeed. Dr Ambedkar, however, knew that they remained only on paper. Discrimination against African Americans resurfaced around 1877 in what is known as 'Black Codes' (forcing African Americans to work only as menial labour) and 'Jim Crow Laws' (forcing African Americans to live in segregated neighbourhoods). And this was widespread during Dr Ambedkar's time in the US and continued even

18 Ibid.

19 Ibid.

thereafter. Why would then Dr Ambedkar be "impressed" by the 14th Amendment to the US Constitution?

* * *

Dr Ambedkar was unquestionably influenced by the life of Booker T. Washington, who was born a slave, strived to get himself educated and then dedicated his life to educating others. But his admiration for Washington ends there. Dr Ambedkar could not have supported Washington's "accommodative" position on the racial problems in the US. Washington's Atlanta Compromise (1895) was widely regarded as his acceptance of segregation and accommodative stance of social policy. "We can be separate as fingers, yet one as the hand, in all things essential to mutual progress," he had said.[20] There is no way that Dr Ambedkar would have appreciated this approach of Booker T. Washington and the person himself.

Intellectually, Dr Ambedkar was closer to the views adopted by William Du Bois. Du Bois was the first African American to earn a doctorate. Similarly, Dr Ambedkar was the first Untouchable to get a PhD in America. However, unlike Booker T Washington, Du Bois fought for full civil rights and increased political participation. Du Bois wanted the African Americans to educate themselves in the best Universities not just for menial work, as encouraged by Washington, so that they could not only compete with the white on equal footing but could also accomplish the much needed social change.

In fact, Dr Ambedkar and Dr Du Bois wrote to each other about their common pursuit of equality and justice. In 1945, Du Bois was part of a three-person delegation representing the NAACP that attended the Conference at which the United Nations (UN) was established. The NAACP delegation wanted the UN to endorse

---

20 Narendra Jadhav, 'India and the US: Caste Race and Economic Growth', Sixth Annual Patrick O'Meara International Lecture (November 2016), Indiana University, Bloomington, USA.

racial equality. On 2 July 1946, Dr Ambedkar wrote to Dr Du Bois exploring the possibility of taking up the question of Untouchability to the newly formed United Nations. He had also asked for a copy of the representation that had been submitted at that time to the United Nations.

Through reply dated 31 July 1946, Dr Du Bois did share the desired document with Dr Ambedkar, but it is not clear what happened next. While Dr Du Bois was getting exasperated "because his efforts to report racist practices in the US as human rights abuses to the newly formed UN were being completely blocked", Dr Ambedkar was completely occupied with the political turmoil leading to the Independence of India. This could perhaps be one of the probable reasons why Dr Ambedkar does not seem to have pursued the issue of Untouchability at the UN.[21]

* * *

Dr Ambedkar and European Thinkers

As discussed before, Dr Ambedkar had read extensively on the entire evolution of liberal and humanitarian thought, right from the Greek thinkers–philosophers up to the liberal political philosophy in the 18th and 19th century England. The common theme of these thoughts was "a sense of importance of human individuality, a liberation of the individual from complete subservience to [any] group and a relaxation of the tight hold of the custom, law and authority...".[22] In other words, "the emergence of liberalism, in the

21 Rajasekhariah A. M., *BR Ambedkar: The Politics of Emancipation,* 1971, p. 11. Both letters are also available in a feature authored by P. Dayanandan on www.roundtable.co.in.

22 As quoted by Khabde, *op cit,* from Encyclopaedia Britanica, Vol. X, p. 848.

broadest sense seeks to protect the individual from arbitrary external restraints that prevent the full realization of his potentialities"[23] and, in his prolific writings and numerous speeches, Dr Ambedkar referenced them, time and again.

Dr Ambedkar quoted Greek historian Thucydides on the first page of his book *What Congress and Gandhi Have Done to Untouchables,* first published in 1945. In the so-called 'Melian Dialogue' reported by Thucydides, Melians said to Athenians before the siege of Melos: "It may be your interest to be our masters, but how can it be in ours to be your slaves."

Dr Ambedkar used this quote, more than once, to instil it in his Untouchable followers, and inspire them to rise and fight for their human rights.

Another Greek work that left an indelible impression upon Dr Ambedkar was the discussion between the two great Greek philosophers Socrates and Thrasymachus.[24] In this discussion, in response to a question by Socrates, Thrasymachus responded: "I proclaim that might is right, and justice is the interest of the stronger .... The different forms of government make laws—democratic, aristocratic, or autocratic—with a view to their respective interests; and these laws, so made by them to serve their interests, they deliver to their subjects as 'justice', and punish as 'unjust' anyone who transgresses them ..."

In Thrasymachus's definition of justice, one can certainly find compassion for the oppressed and depressed classes of any society. As such, this discussion, arguably, may have sowed the seeds of Republicanism in the mind of Dr Ambedkar.

* * *

23 Ibid.

24 Will Durant, *The Story of Philosophy* (New York: Schuster, 1926). The quote here is from the 1957 edition, p. 16.

Dr Ambedkar had also studied the European history thoroughly. He had read extensively about the Renaissance (1300–1600) which saw the transition of Europe from the Middle Ages to Modernity on to the Protestant Reformation (1517–1648) which challenged the Roman Catholic Church and Pope's authority, and further on to the French Revolution (1789–1799).

In all these studies, Dr Ambedkar consistently directed his interest towards the suppressed and oppressed people worldwide. It's not surprising that while writing or speaking about the Untouchables in India, he frequently drew parallels to historical contexts such as the Romans and their slaves, Spartans and their Helots (a class of serfs with status between slaves and citizens), and British and their villeins (tenants or serfs who provided dues and services to the lord of the manor in return for land in the feudal system)[25].

From the post-Protestant Reformation period, Dr Ambedkar was greatly influenced by the thoughts of the French philosopher and historian Voltaire. His entire life, Voltaire had conflicts with the Popes and Catholic orthodoxy. He wrote quite sarcastically, "Christianity must be divine, since it has lasted 1,700 years despite the fact that it is so full of villainy and nonsense. All ancient people had myths and they are invented by priests."[26]

Will Durant has quoted Voltaire addressing common masses: "Men fed by your labours in a comfortable idleness, enriched by your sweat and your misery struggled for partisans and slaves. They inspired you with a destructive fanaticism that they might be your masters. They made you superstitious, not that you might fear God, but that you might fear them."[27]

25 Ambedkar, *Mr Gandhi and Emancipation of Untouchables*, p. 12.

26 Khabde, *op cit,* from Encyclopaedia Britanica, Vol. X, p. 121.

27 Durant, *The Story of Philosophy* (1957) p. 215.

Dr Ambedkar questioned as to why no Brahmin scholar had come forward to play the role of Voltaire? He said: "No Brahmin scholar came forward to play the part of Voltaire who had the intellectual honesty to rise against the doctrines of the Catholic Church in which he was brought up ... It is a grave reflection on the scholarship of the Brahmins that they should not have produced a Voltaire."[28]

Dr Ambedkar drew from Voltaire when he argued that: "Hindu civilization, gauged in the light of these social products (i.e., Casteism and Untouchability), could hardly be called a civilization. [It is] a diabolical contrivance to suppress and enslave humanity and its proper name would be infamy."

* * *

Another thinker that profoundly influenced Dr Ambedkar was Edmund Burke, an Irish Statesman and Philosopher (1729-1797).

Dr Ambedkar regarded Edmund Burke as a great teacher of political philosophy. No wonder there are many similarities in their beliefs and expression. Both Burke and Ambedkar were icons of humanity, justice and moral order. Both always advocated for the upliftment of suppressed people. Both highlighted the importance of spirit and principles of morality into the conduct of public affairs. Both strongly campaigned for the moral regeneration of society through educating the public opinion.

Burke had said:

> The use of force alone is but temporary. It may endure for a moment; but does not remove the necessity of subduing again, and a nation is not governed which is perpetually to be conquered .... A further objection to force is that you impair the object by your very endeavours to preserve it. The thing you

28 Ambedkar B.R., *The Untouchables*, (first published in 1948) BAWS Vol. 7, Preface.

> fought for is not the thing which you recover; but depreciated, sunk, wasted and consumed in the context.[29]

Dr Ambedkar referenced this quote from Burke at least twice: first, at the Round Table Conference in London in 1931, imploring the British authorities not to resort to force in turning down the demands of Depressed Classes in India and second, in the Constituent Assembly debates, while addressing the Hindu-Muslim problem.

* * *

Dr Ambedkar held in great regard the British philosopher, political economist and civil servant, John Stuart Mill (1806-1873). With his colossal book titled *On Liberty*, first published in 1859, Mill was widely regarded as the philosophical leader of the British liberalism.

Mill's *On Liberty* is a philosophical essay which sets down standards for the relationship between the authority (such as Government) and individual liberty. Mill cautions that democratic ideals may lead to the "tyranny of the majority".

In the essay, Mill argues *inter alia:* "... there needs to be protection also against the tyranny of the prevailing opinion and feeling; against the tendency of society to impose, by other means than civil penalties, its own ideas and practices as rules of conduct on those who dissent from them; ... ."

According to Mill, "There is a limit to the legitimate interference of collective opinion with individual independence, and to find that limit and maintain it against encroachment, is as dispensable to a good condition of human affairs as protection against political despotism."

---

29 Burke, Edmunds, *Reflection on the Revolution in France*, first published in 1790.

Building on Mill's argument of the "tyranny of the majority", Dr Ambedkar pointed out:

> In India, the majority is not a political majority. In India, majority is born, it is not made [as in European democracies]. There is a difference between a communal majority and a political majority. A political majority is not a fixed or a permanent majority. It is a majority which is always made, unmade and remade. [On the other hand] a communal majority is a permanent majority fixed in its attitude .... If there is so much objection [in terms of the tyranny] to a political majority, how very fatal must it be the objection to a communal majority.[30]

Again, while addressing the Constituent Assembly, Dr Ambedkar said: "... in the name of democracy, there must be no tyranny of the majority over minority. The minority must always feel safe although the majority is carrying on the government, the minority is not being hurt or the minority is not being hit below the belt."

Dr Ambedkar strongly advocated that the Indian Constitution must contain checks and balances to prevent tyranny by communal majority against the Depressed Classes. He forcefully argued in favour of provisions safeguarding the interests of the minorities from tyranny of the majority.

Once more, while addressing the Constituent Assembly, Dr Ambedkar quoted Mill. In order to maintain democracy not simply outwardly, but also in substance, *inter alia*, Dr Ambedkar argued that: "... we must do is to observe the caution which John Stuart Mill has given to all who are interested in the maintenance of democracy, namely, not to lay their liberties at the feet of even a

---

30 Ambedkar, *Annihilation of Caste*, first published in 1936, BAWS Vol. 1.

great man, or to trust him with powers which enable him to subvert their institutions."

When it came to patriotism, Dr Ambedkar would often quote the Irish political leader Daniel O'Connell (1775–1847) who famously said, "No man can be grateful at the cost of his honour, no woman can be grateful at the cost of her chastity and no nation can be grateful at the cost of its liberty."

* * *

Amongst the then contemporary thinkers who influenced Dr Ambedkar was Prof. Harold J. Laski (1893–1950),[31] who was a British political theorist and economist. Dr Ambedkar was very moved by Laski's view: "The moral order is always taken for granted in democracy. If there was no moral order, democracy will go to pieces."[32]

Dr Ambedkar argued along these lines on multiple occasions. According to him, the majority of the people are left to be governed not so much by the law as by morality. Law plays a miniscule role in human activity, where there is dispute and disorder.

* * *

In a public speech in 1954, Dr Ambedkar stated that he has had three *Gurus*. He said: "I am a devotee of Gautam Buddha, Kabir and Mahatma Phule and worshipper of learning, self-respect and character."[33]

---

31 According to Keer, Prof. Harold J. Laski was actually present when Dr Ambedkar read a paper at the London School of Economics. However, there is no independent confirmation.

32 Harold J. Laski, *A Grammar of Politics* (London: George Allen & Unwin Ltd, 1925). Also quoted by Khabde, *op cit.*

33 Marathi Speech. For English translation, see Jadhav, Narendra (2013), *op cit,* Vol. I, p. 58.

Dr Ambedkar remained a keen student and life-long learner all his life. A great book-lover, collector and of course, an exceptionally sharp avid reader, he was perhaps the only person in the world who built a house simply for storing his vast book collection.[34]

As a lifelong worshipper of learning, Dr Ambedkar studied a very wide range of Western thinkers that ranged from Socrates (470 BC–399 BC) to Harold J. Laski (1893–1950), especially on the subject of the evolution of liberal and humanitarian thought.

As a result, Dr Ambedkar emerged as an intellectual colossus, a great thought leader and a universal defender of human rights, whose political philosophy comprised of liberal thinking and the spirit of Republicanism.

34 'Rajgruha', his personal residence in Mumbai, built around 1934.

PART II

Dr Ambedkar: The Liberal Republicanism in Action

CHAPTER FOUR

Laying Foundation of a Mass Movement

Back home in India, Dr Ambedkar encountered challenges in supporting his household, which included his wife, child and several dependant relatives. In June 1923, he registered at the Bombay High Court (on the Appellate side) to begin his law practice. The expenses associated with acquiring an office near the High Court in South Mumbai posed a deterrent. However, with the assistance from friends, Dr Ambedkar set up an office at Damodar Hall in Parel. Getting clients proved difficult, as the so-called high-Caste Hindus were reluctant to entrust him with cases. However, after several months, he got his first case. To sustain himself, in 1925, he applied for and began teaching Mercantile Law part-time, earning a salary of Rs 200 per month and additional fees as an examiner for Bombay University.

Bahishkrit Hitakarini Sabha

On 9 March 1924, Dr Ambedkar set out to launch a mass movement by founding a social organization for the Depressed Classes, which he named the *Bahishkrit Hitakarini Sabha,* where he assumed the role of Chairman of its Managing Committee.[1] The organization's slogan, 'Educate, Organize and Agitate', was going to reverberate throughout India for decades to come.

The *Sabha* aimed to: promote education, *inter alia,* by opening hostels; foster cultural advancement through libraries and study circles; create job opportunities by starting Industrial and Agricultural Schools;[2] and advocate for the grievances of the Depressed Classes. It commenced its operations with a small library in Parel, Mumbai, and a hostel for Depressed Class students in Solapur in January 1925. Rallies and meetings were regularly conducted across the Bombay Presidency.

In his early speeches, Dr Ambedkar outlined his mission and defined his role. At a social workers' meeting in Mumbai on 9 March 1924, which led to the establishment of *Bahishkrit Hitakarini Sabha,* Dr Ambedkar proclaimed:

> I would certainly not limit the use of the power of my intellect only to my family and my Caste. I will render them to the benefit of entire Depressed Classes, to help them build their social movement and struggle.
>
> The challenges lying before the Untouchables are formidable. I am aware that I may not be able to solve all their problems. But I am confident that I can pose these challenges before the world and bring our agony to their notice. The challenges before the Untouchables are like the mighty Himalayas. I am going to bang my head against these Himalayas. So please remember that even if I am not able to bring down the Himalayas, seven crore

---

1 A number of highly distinguished 'Touchables' were office-bearers, namely, Sir Chimanlal Setalvad (President) and Dr R. P. Paranjpye as well as B. G. Kher as Vice Presidents (Fifteen years later Shri B. G. Kher became the Chief Minister for the Bombay Province).

2 This is reminiscent of the work done by Booker T. Washington for African American youth in the US in the late 19th and early 20th Centuries.

> [70 million] Untouchables, on witnessing my bloodied head, would be ready to sacrifice their lives to bring the Himalayas down. However, if you continue to encourage hostile feelings among yourselves, then not only I, but even God, will not be able to help you.

Dr Ambedkar's speeches were not only inspiring and stirring but also had the power to evoke self-respect among the Depressed Classes and promote political awareness. "Lack of collective willpower is holding us back," he emphasized. On 1 January 1927, during a meeting at Koregaon War Memorial[3] near Pune, Dr Ambedkar recounted to his Untouchable *Mahar* followers the "tenacious and courageous fight" waged by their forefathers. Dr Ambedkar later reminded them: "We are no slaves. We are a warrior clan. Nothing is more disgraceful for a brave man than to live a life devoid of self-respect and without the love for the country."[4]

---

3 Marathi Speech; Meeting at the Koregaon War Memorial, Koregaon near Pune, (1 January 1927). English Report: BAWS Vol.17 (3), pp. 3-7.
Koregaon War Memorial is an obelisk—65 feet high, standing on a stone platform of about 32 sq. ft. The War Memorial was erected by the British to commemorate mostly *Mahar* soldiers who "fought tenaciously and with magnificent courage" in a great fight on 1 January 1818 between the British forces—very small in number, led by Capt. Stawton and the Army of Peshwa Bajirao II led by General Gokhale, which was several times larger in size. The British forces, comprising mostly of *Mahar* soldiers "fought without rest or respite, food or water, continuously for twelve hours". This action of "heroic valour and enduring fortitude" displaying "disciplined intrepidity" and "devoted courage and admirable constancy" won great renown for the *Mahar* soldiers. The names of the *Mahar* soldiers killed and wounded have been inscribed on the Monument.

4 A major incident occurred at Bhima Koregaon on 1 January 2018, where violence erupted during the annual celebratory event to mark the 200th anniversary of the Battle of Bhima Koregaon victory.

Importantly, Dr Ambedkar clearly articulated his vision for the Untouchables within the framework of *Swaraj* (Home-rule) early on (24 May 1924) asserting, "If *Swaraj* is coming, we must get equal political rights in it".

Underlining how Untouchability is more deplorable than slavery, he said:[5]

> ... History is replete with examples wherein slaves were liberated and then became independent citizens of the State. But there is not a single example in India, where Untouchables became Touchable. Roman slavery was time bound and there were many ways to get liberated from it. On the contrary, Untouchability (in India) is eternal and there is no way to get liberated from it. Because of the strict rule that an Untouchable is Untouchable by birth, centuries have passed and yet the situation has not changed at all. Untouchability is several times a greater hurdle in the path of progress of the Untouchables in India, than slavery was for Romans ....

In the same speech, Dr Ambedkar discussed various options for the Depressed Classes to come out of Untouchability, including mass conversion to another religion. He said:

> ... Sometimes, we are told that Untouchables should migrate to another country altogether .... But it is not possible for all our people to migrate. Very few people would be able to do it. Therefore, we must search for ways of eradication of Untouchability, by staying in the confines of this country.
>
> The second option is that of Conversion. We should look at

5 Marathi Speech, Conference of Depressed Classes from Bombay Province, Barshi, District Solapur (24 May 1924). For English translation, see *Ambedkar Speaks* (ed. Jadhav, Narendra, 2013), *op cit,* Vol. III, pp. 49-53.

> any religion with rationality and pragmatism. In the context of philosophy, the Hindu religion is as good as any other religion, even better. 'There is the same soul in all human beings'—is the fundamental principle of Hindu philosophy. If our social constitution was in reality, actually a reflection of this noble thought, then Hindus would have definitely treated all citizens with equal respect. However, this has not happened .... Where is the convergence between thought and action? We worship and uphold the same Vedic philosophy and yet, they hate us. Not only that, they treat us lower than even animals. Why respect a religion which does not respect human beings? Why stick to religion which keeps us away from material prosperity and pushes us in to despair and despondency?...

In the course of his speech, Dr Ambedkar heartily welcomed the possibility of attaining the Independence. He said:

> ... British Government had decided not to interfere in the Caste System and Customs. In this context, a welcome development is the possibility to attaining Independence for our country.
>
> Our people are somehow afraid of the Independence, and they feel *Peshwa* rule [Brahmin-*raj*] will return after the Independence. It must be remembered that there is a big difference. *Peshwa* did not rule with consent of people; they ruled by hereditary regimes. It wasn't peoples' rule. In future, no State will rule without the consent of the people. *Swaraj* with the consent of people at large is the best possible political system.
>
> If Independence is attained, then we must get equal rights as everyone else, and to achieve that we must secure the right to vote. Today right to vote is so limited that only about two per cent people are qualified to vote. Securing the right to vote will help us in two ways. One the Legislative Council will no longer ignore our plight. Those people who get elected because of our votes, will not be able to overlook our interests. Moreover, it will

> no longer be possible to maintain the *Varnashram Dharma*. If a Brahmin has to beg for votes from Untouchables, what would remain of the *Varnashram Dharma*? It will also be a great assault on the Caste System.

Dr Ambedkar underscored the need for an organization of Untouchables. He said:

> ... It is not enough to keep complaining about. We should make conscious efforts aimed at increasing capability of our people. If there is equality in virtues then the Caste-based discrimination and Untouchability will disappear over time.
>
> From the viewpoint of our country, these are extra-ordinary times. The process of laying of the foundation of *Swaraj* began in 1917. Since then this country has witnessed formation of three groups: (1) European, (2) *Musalman*, (3) Hindu. Before 1917, Muslims had a volatile relationship with Hindus but that has been reversed. Together, both have taken their own share from British in the form of independence. But now there are tensions between the two groups. Issue that has been agitating their minds is which community gets a larger share of the incipient *Swaraj*. Obviously, the group with a larger population would get proportionately larger share.
>
> In this struggle the spotlight is increasingly coming to Untouchables. Both groups have realized the importance of number that we have. If we continue to remain Hindus, then alone this country will be able to perpetuate the Aryan culture. On the other hand, if we convert ourselves to Islam, this country will have dominance of Islamic culture.
>
> Both Hindus and Muslims seem to recognize this fully well ... Although we are at the rock bottom of the Indian society, in this conflict of cultures (that is, Aryan v/s Islamic), our numbers are critical and, therefore, if we create organizational strength, we certainly would have a great bargaining power.

While concluding, Dr Ambedkar made an earnest appeal to his followers. He said:

> Our community is backward in all respects. Financially it is weak; it is lacking in confidence.... [we] are lost in ignorance, and ... are at complete loss of direction in ... lives. That is precisely why those who do understand this grave situation and those who have a sense of duty must come forward and selflessly devote themselves to the betterment of Untouchable masses.
>
> My educated Brothers, if you want your future generations to remember you with respect and regards, if you want the condition of your children and grandchildren to be better than the situation that you have been in, please do come forward. It is your solemn duty to do ... very best so as to rectify the situation.

An examination of these early speeches, during which Dr Ambedkar was still laying the foundation of his mission, reveals an underlying theme of Republicanism.

CHAPTER FIVE

Commencing the Mass Movement

As the mass movement spearheaded by Dr Ambedkar started to pick up momentum, his personal challenges on the family front seemed unending. The most devastating blow occurred in July 1926 when his newborn child, named Rajratna, passed away.

The situation took a favourable turn in December 1926 when Dr Ambedkar was nominated as a Member of Bombay Legislative Council (BLC). Under the Government of India Act, 1919, provision was made for one Nominated Member to represent the Depressed Classes. Dr Ambedkar tried to convince the British Government to increase the number of Nominated Members representing the Depressed Classes in the Province, a demand that was accepted. In December 1926, the number for the Bombay Provincial Council was doubled to two, and Dr Ambedkar, along with Dr P. G. Solanki, was nominated to this Council. This marked the beginning of Dr Ambedkar's illustrious career as a legislator.

In the Bombay Provincial Council

As a nominated Member of the BLC, Dr Ambedkar quickly garnered the respect of his colleagues for his diligent, analytical and thorough interventions. In his inaugural speech at the BLC on 24 February

1927, Dr Ambedkar focused on the Provincial Budget for 1927-28. He criticized the existing revenue system for its lack of reliability. He also lamented over the limited degree of freedom the House possessed, with only 40 per cent control over revenue and 64 per cent over expenditure. He also rebuked the Government for the significant rise in unproductive expenditure, which led to large budget deficit.

At the Council, Dr Ambedkar consistently drew attention to the importance of both School and Higher Education. Addressing the issue of School Education on 12 March 1927, Dr Ambedkar highlighted the necessity to increase per capita expenditure on education. He also emphasized the importance of establishing an inspecting agency to ensure that educational bodies did not neglect the needs of Depressed Classes.

Dr Ambedkar played a major role in the debate on the Bombay University Act (Amendment) Bill. Dr Ambedkar pointed out that "one of the greatest defects from which this (i.e., Bombay) University has suffered ever since it was established was that it was primarily constituted as an examining body".

He analysed the proposals before the Council and made suggestions that would help the University of Bombay into becoming a better teaching University, promoting Higher Education and Research.

* * *

Dr Ambedkar's appointment to the BLC provided a framework for his strategy to initiate a mass movement for the emancipation of Untouchables. Clearly, in the initial stage, which lasted for nearly a decade, Dr Ambedkar focused on advocating for social justice while remaining within the fold of the Hindu religion. His approach aimed to frame the mass movement as a struggle for civic rights for the Untouchables.

The initial action taken towards this goal was a simple demand to obtain drinking water from a public reservoir, which took place in the small town of Mahad in Konkan. This demand was about asserting one's fundamental right to water for Untouchables.

For centuries, Untouchables were barred from accessing water from places where the Upper Castes collected it. In 1926, the Government of Bombay Province passed a resolution prohibiting such discriminatory practices. On account of the same, the Mahad Municipality adopted a resolution granting Untouchables full access to all water bodies, including the largest reservoir, the Chavdar Lake. However, this resolution failed to translate into tangible access, and Hindu Untouchables were still denied the right to draw water from the lake. In contrast, no such restriction existed for Muslim and Christian Untouchables. The plight of the Hindu Untouchables was even worse than that of the cattle belonging to the High Caste, which were taken to Chavdar Lake. This injustice became Dr Ambedkar's launchpad for his revolution.

Chavdar Lake Struggle

Dr Ambedkar convened a gathering in Mahad, where the Untouchables would assert their right *en masse*. On 19 March 1927, the *Bahishkrit Hitakarini Sabha* organized a Conference of Depressed Classes in Mahad. Responding to Dr Ambedkar's call, people turned out in huge numbers. Thousands, across all age groups, mostly dressed in tatters and carrying *bhakris* (round flat bread popular in Maharashtra and Gujarat) wrapped in cloth bags, came together from different parts of the Province.

During this landmark meeting, Dr Ambedkar first demonstrated how the British had failed to uplift the Untouchables and exhorted the assembly to keep alive the (new) fire of awareness.

Dr Ambedkar then elaborated the essentials for the progress of Untouchables. He said:[1]

> Gentlemen, it is my opinion that Government always neglects us because we are cooperative .... We blame our fate for all kinds of problems. Sooner we discard this suicidal attitude, the better.
>
> In my opinion two things are essential for the progress of Untouchables. First, the rust of retrograde thoughts of inferiority accumulated in their minds must be cleaned up. Unless the attitude, thoughts and speech are cleaned, the seeds of awakening and progress cannot take roots in the minds of Untouchables. In the present circumstances nothing can grow on the hard rocks of their mind ....

Dr Ambedkar added:

> ...Today, amongst Untouchables, *Mahars* are like a herd of useless people. They have developed a habit of living on State food begged from house to house. They do it as if it is their great right; begging door to door for State food. As a result, nobody respects them. They have lost their self-respect and dignity. They have lost their independence and cannot take a path of progress. If they think of entering temple, or attempt to draw water from public place, or decide not to carry dead animals, the next day they lose their State food. It is most shameful to sell your humanity for a few State crumbs ....
>
> Whenever, any progressive steps are discussed, 'our elder's custom is better' is the kind of approach of people in this area. Their attitude is that the old custom may be highly detrimental but must be followed. But don't you think that every parent wants that his children should live better than him at least, a

1 For fuller version of the speech, see, Jadhav, Narendra (2013), *Ambedkar Speaks,* op cit, Vol. III, pp. 55-60.

> little better? If they do not think so then what is the difference between them and animals?

After inspiring the gathering to resist the humiliating and enslaving custom of village duties, Dr Ambedkar proceeded to make an ardent appeal. He said:

> Gentlemen, if not for you, at least for the sake of your children please listen to what I say. You may ask, 'why do all these difficult things when you are comfortable, maybe on half a bread.' You may ask me, 'why leave assured half bread for an imaginary full bread.' But I must warn you, if you do not do what I tell, you will not get even this half bread in times to come.
>
> I want to emphasize that we all have to undertake this work of social awareness very enthusiastically.... You must not let this fire of awakening douse.

* * *

The first day of the Conference was a display of strength. Dr Ambedkar's speech had a palpable impact on the crowd. Several resolutions were passed that day, including the decision that the Untouchables would not bury the dead cattle of the Touchables and that they should do it themselves. Moreover, the resolution granting all Untouchables access to all waterfronts should be enforced.

On the second day (i.e. 20 March 1927), as the Conference was nearing its conclusion, a local Touchable Hindu leader Shri Anantrao Chitre suddenly rose from the crowd (as per the strategy) and declared: "Let's go to Chavdar Lake and implement the Mahad Municipality Resolution."

And thus began the famous march!

More than 10,000 people followed Dr Ambedkar to Chavdar Lake, marching in a disciplined manner in rows of four, shouting slogans: "Educate, Unite, and Agitate"! The reservoir was situated amidst the homes of the Upper Castes. Stunned faces peered through every door, window, and terrace of every house to witness the massive, determined crowd gathered around their tank, "polluting" its purity.

After reaching the Chavdar Tank, Dr Ambedkar descended the half-dozen steps with determination. Facing the thousands of expectant followers, he calmly bent down, scooped water in his hands, and drank. There was a huge uproar and the crowd chanted *Dr Ambedkar ki jay!* (Victory to Dr Ambedkar!) as everyone symbolically sipped water from the Chavdar Tank. A revolution had begun.

Dr Ambedkar then proclaimed to the exuberant crowd that the Untouchables were asserting their rights as equal human beings and rewriting history.

Shortly thereafter, a horde of Upper Castes armed with bamboo sticks congregated at street corners, catching the Untouchables off guard. Rumours circulated that the Untouchables were planning to forcibly enter the local temple. The horde attacked the delegates, who fled in panic. They made no distinction between men, women or children. The protestors were charged with fury, ready to retaliate at Dr Ambedkar's command. Mahad seemed to be on the brink of turning into a battleground. However, Dr Ambedkar directed them to maintain peace and discipline. He reinforced that their struggle was to "uphold the law, not to break it".

* * *

The "Mahad March" was a pivotal moment. It was for the first time that the Depressed Classes had collectively and publicly attempted to reclaim the civic rights that had been denied to them for ages.

Dr Ambedkar emerged as the messiah of the downtrodden, igniting within them the flame of self-respect and self-elevation. As a direct consequence of the Mahad Conference, many Untouchables immediately abandoned practices such as eating carrion and skinning carcasses, while others stopped begging for crumbs.[2]

* * *

Bahishkrit Hitakarini Sabha convened another meeting in Mumbai on 3 July 1927, in response to the oppression faced in Mahad. Dr Ambedkar announced his plan to do a *Satyagraha* in Mahad, stating, "We need bold and self-respecting people for *Mahad Satyagraha*."

While Mahad *Satyagraha* was gaining ground, some Untouchable activists initiated a Temple Entry *Satyagraha* in Ambadevi Temple at Amravati, located in the Vidarbha region of Maharashtra. At the same time, a Conference of the Untouchables from Berar (i.e., Vidarbha) was organized in Amravati.

In his Presidential Address on 13 November 1927, Dr Ambedkar expounded on his philosophy behind the *Satyagraha* movement.[3] He said:

> The Untouchables and Touchables both agree that they both belong to the same religion. The Touchables never tell Untouchables that they are not Hindus....
>
> Both the parties since ancient times feel that they belong to the same religion. However, today there is great change in the outlook of Untouchables, as is clearly visible. They are wondering if they are also Hindus why they do not have the same rights like the other Hindus? Why cannot they draw water from the same well or lake which is used by other Hindus? Why

---

2 At this point of time, Dr Ambedkar started a new fortnightly, titled: *Bahishkrut Bharat* and began responding to critics of his mass movement and explaining his point of view to general public.

3 For full English summary, see (ed. Jadhav, Narendra, 2013), *op cit*, *Ambedkar Speaks*, Vol I, pp. 93-101.

can't they enter the temple where Hindus worship their Gods? They are asking these questions of equality. They are insisting on getting these equal rights....

The behaviour of Hindus is rather very amusing; that is so long as somebody is a part of Hindu society, the barbarous rule of Untouchability, sin and virtue, significance-insignificance are applied to them. If he leaves the Hindu religion then these rules cease to operate; he is treated with equality. That is the reason why Hindus do not consider Muslims as Untouchables. They do not consider even animals such as cats and goats to be Untouchables. Untouchables are part of Hindu religion and that is why their barbarous rules are applied to them.

Untouchables know it well that if any Untouchable gets converted to another religion like Islam or Christianity he is treated with humanity, with equality. Still Untouchables do not want to follow this simple path. *Instead of abandoning the Hindu religion and causing its decline, they want to remain within the Hindu religion and use all their energy to fight for the rights of humanity.* [emphasis added] They are *not* demanding any special rights and status; they are demanding only equal treatment.... Their demand is only for equal rights with the Touchables. Now, if you apply the principles of Gita, you will find that this movement of Untouchables is a movement for *Satyagraha.*

* * *

The Chavdar Lake March had stirred the Untouchables to action. However, on 4 August 1927, they faced a setback when the Mahad Municipality retracted its previous resolution granting the Untouchables access to the water tank. Dr Ambedkar saw this as a challenge and declared his intention to escalate the struggle by convening another protest meeting in Mahad.

The Mahad Satyagraha

A larger crowd gathered in December 1927 in Mahad. Dr Ambedkar announced that the Mahad *Satyagraha* was just the beginning for laying the foundation of equality.[4] He said:

> Many of you would recollect that we had together gone to the Mahad Chawdar Lake on the March 19. Although, the Touchables had not objected to our going there, they registered their objection by assaulting the Untouchables later on.
>
> This water lake of Mahad is a public property. The Touchables of Mahad are so generous that they allow to draw water by all the people; even the Muslims and persons of other religions also are free to draw water from there. Not only that, they do not have objection to even animals to drink water from this lake. They allow all animals even those belonging to the Untouchables.
>
> The Touchables of Mahad are opposing Untouchables to draw water from Mahad Lake not because its water will get polluted or it will vanish in the thin air. They oppose it because they do not want to accept that the Untouchables are equal to them. Gentlemen, you will understand the significance of the movement of *Satyagraha that* we have launched ....
>
> Our objective is to prove that we are human beings just like others. Therefore, this Conference is arranged to lay a foundation for establishing the social equality. And, therefore, this Conference is unique and historical. There is no parallel to this event in the entire history of India.

Dr Ambedkar clarified that the Conference was comparable to Versailles Conference in France (May 1789). Explaining about the French Conference, he said:

---

4 For details, see *Ambedkar Speaks* (ed. Jadhav, Narendra, 2013), *op cit,* Vol I, pp. 93-101.

The Third Declaration [of the Versailles Conference] was the most important declaration; rather a King of all Declarations. It was later known as Declaration of the Fundamental Rights throughout the world. It created revolutionary changes in France and in all the countries in Europe and also elsewhere.

It has 17 Articles of which the following are important:

(a) All persons are born equal and remain of equal status till death.

(b) The polity of the nation must always ensure that these human rights are protected.

(c) People are the supreme authority to grant any authority or powers. No authority of any community or person shall be valid unless it is granted by people. There shall be no other basis, whether political or religious, for getting such authority.

(d) Every person has complete freedom of behaviour as per his Fundamental Rights. If there are to be any restrictions on him those will be to ensure that others' Fundamental Rights are not violated and such restrictions shall be imposed only by law. These restrictions shall not be imposed on the basis of religion or any other consideration.

(e) The law will impose only such restrictions as may be necessary for social harmony.

(f) Law shall be made by the People or their duly elected representatives. All laws whether these are protective or punitive shall be equally applicable to every citizen. All people shall be equally eligible for respect, honour, human rights or profession. There shall be no restrictions on the basis of birth, sex, caste or creed.

We should remember these principles of Versailles Conference for this Mahad Conference of ours. This Conference should follow the same path and same programmes to dismantle the frames of *Varnashram* in Hinduism; *we should adopt the programmes for unifying all the five Varnas and to form only one solid Class of all the Hindus* [emphasis added]. Unless it is done, the Untouchability will not vanish and there will be no equality and fraternity in our society.

* * *

Burning of Manusmriti

Dr Ambedkar questioned the authority of all Hindu Scriptures. He asked, "If you say your religion is our religion, your rights and ours must be equal. Is this the case? If not, on what grounds do you say that we must remain in the Hindu fold?"

Dr Ambedkar condemned the *Manusmriti*. This book contained the rules governing the lives of Hindus. Revered by the so-called Upper-Caste Hindus but detested by the Untouchables, it contained instructions such as pouring molten lead into the ears of Untouchables if they heard or read the sacred *Vedas*. Dr Ambedkar denounced the *Manusmriti* as a Charter of slavery for the Untouchables and labelled it a symbol of tyranny among the Hindus. He then called for the public burning of copies of the Holy Book.

On 25 December 1927, a copy of the *Manusmriti* was placed on a special pyre and ceremoniously burned as the Untouchables cheered on. This bold gesture established that the Untouchables were no longer willing to be held hostage by the religious and ritual confinements propagated by the Caste Hindus.

* * *

[*The next day i.e., 26 December 1927, the Conference was converted into a Committee so as to pass resolutions about the movement. Accordingly, Dr Ambedkar advised the volunteers not to allow any outsider in the hall. Then Dr Ambedkar put up the following proposal.*]

Dr Ambedkar said:

> ...*Satyagraha* is a difficult test of persistence. You will have to observe very strong restraint on yourself.... (1) No sticks to be carried; (2) Follow Government orders; (3) Be ready to go to the jail; and (4) Do not seek pardon for doing *Satyagraha*.
>
> You must strictly follow these rules. Then only you can participate in the *Satyagraha*. Do not join the movement because I am telling you. Our fight is for the justice. If you are convinced and you are ready for facing the troubles and difficulties then only join the *Satyagraha*.

[After his speech Dr Ambedkar requested others to speak 'For' and 'Against' the proposal].

Considering that a majority of people was in favour of the *Satyagraha,* the Collector was invited to address the gathering. The Collector spoke about prohibitory orders of the court and advised the people to desist from participating in the *Satyagraha*.

After the Collector left, people again spoke in favour of *Satyagraha*. After discussions amongst few selected leaders, it was decided that the *Satyagraha* be deferred for the time being. Instead a rally should be taken in Mahad around the lake. Accordingly, the Collector was informed in the late evening.

[*Later, the assembly led a massive rally on the roads of Mahad and passed it encircling the lake. It was so huge that it took more than two hours at such a small place. It was very disciplined. The Touchable Hindus were afraid to step out of their houses and all shops were shut. Although Satyagrahis did not actually enter the Mahad Lake, they had literally captured it by surrounding it on all sides.*]

Ironically, following the Chavdar Lake struggle earlier, the orthodox Caste Hindus of Mahad had the Brahmin priests "purify" the "desecrated" reservoir by pouring into it 108 pots of curd, milk, cow dung and cow urine amid loud religious chanting!

By burning the Hindu scriptures at the same place only a few months later, Dr Ambedkar had cemented the fight for the right to drinking water into a socio-cultural movement for equality of the downtrodden masses.

* * *

Around this time (December 1927) Dr Ambedkar founded the *Samata Sainik Dal* (Social Equality Corps) with the objective of aggressively pursuing the agenda of social equality.

CHAPTER SIX

Escalating the Mass Movement

In 1928, the *Bahishkrit Hitakarini Sabha* was dissolved, and a new organization, the Depressed Classes Education Society, was created for spreading education among these marginalized segments of society.

During 1928 and 1929, Dr Ambedkar, after the reverberations of the Mahad *Satyagraha,* delivered several crucial speeches. In one notable address, he remarked:[1]

> Primarily there are three objections raised against our movement. First one is that we run a separate movement and don't co-operate with Caste Hindus. Second objection is that our stance is aggressive. Third objection is that we unnecessary complicate two entirely different issues: Untouchability and Casteism, and treat them as one. This is unnecessarily delaying the eradication of Untouchability, it is said.
>
> Those who accuse us of being aggressive should be ashamed of themselves. There is no other community in the world as

---

1 For full English Summary, see *Ambedkar Speaks* (ed. Jadhav, Narendra), *op cit,* Vol. I, p.11. The original Marathi speech was delivered in a Ganesh Festival in Mumbai (25 September 1928).

> modest as Untouchable.... Haven't we remained meek under the most humiliating and inhuman circumstances, for ages?....

Answering to the third objection, Dr Ambedkar said, "I want to tell you that our movement for Untouchability eradication is not limited to only Untouchable Class but aspires to destroy the hereditary Untouchability in the Hindu Society."

In another speech,[2] Dr Ambedkar told his followers:

> Your worth is not recognized only because you are born in a particular Untouchable Caste; even though you might be well qualified, very intelligent and efficient. Therefore, we will have to adopt aggressive methods to establish our rights. Unless we do it, our efforts would be futile. Another method to remove the injustice caused to us is to capture the power. We need to have the political power to dismantle this frame of *Chaturvana* and get an entry into politics.[3]

In another speech, Dr Ambedkar minced no words, asserting that unless the Depressed Classes declared war on oppression, they would remain deprived of their human rights.[4]

* * *

History is replete with stories of thought leaders—who believe in bringing about a change through the law-making process—or activists those who believe in bringing about a change through mass

---

2 For English Summary, see *Ambedkar Speaks* (ed. Narendra Jadhav), *op cit,* Vol. III, pp. 64-65. The original Marathi speech was delivered at Social Conference of Depressed Classes, in Belgaum.

3 Dr Ambedkar formally joined politics much later, in 1936.

4 Presidential Address (Marathi) in Chitegaon, Nashik (June 21, 1929).

movements. In Dr Ambedkar, one can see a perfect blend of these two traits. Dr Ambedkar was a great scholar, who was respected as an Economic Administrator and was often nominated to Government committees and posts. At the same time, Dr Ambedkar was also a mass leader who led people through the streets. Dr Ambedkar excelled in both these roles striving for social justice for the downtrodden, in the classical Republican spirit.

Temple Entry Satyagraha

Inspired by the Mahad *Satyagraha*, there were two Temple Entry *Satyagraha* efforts in 1929—one in Kali Temple, Khulana, Bengal (8 July 1929) and another one in Parvati Temple, Poona (now known as Pune) around the same time.

Parvati Temple Satyagraha

A public meeting was organized in Mumbai to extend support to 'Parvati *Satyagraha* in Poona' (16 October 1929). In that meeting, Dr Ambedkar explained in brief a history of *Satyagraha* in Poona and emphasized that it is the pious duty of every person from the Depressed Classes to support this *Satyagraha* in every possible way.

Dr Ambedkar said:

> There are people who are advising the Depressed Classes to wait and watch for the change in the attitude of the Upper Castes. What a deplorable advice! On one hand, the Congress has given an ultimatum to British that if the Dominion Status is not granted by December 31, (1929), they will sever all relations with the British Government. And on the other hand, these people are advising the Depressed Classes to wait and watch for getting human rights and social freedom. I wonder if this is not a deception!...

Kala Ram Temple Satyagraha

Dr Ambedkar sustained the momentum of his mass movement for social cause through a temple entry agitation at the Kala Ram Temple in Nashik.[5] On 1 March 1930, the Untouchables from all over Maharashtra were called to Nashik to assert their right to worship Lord Ram at the Kala Ram Temple. In response to Dr Ambedkar's appeal, thousands flocked to Nashik. The mass movement led by Dr Ambedkar was gaining traction.

Addressing the public gathering, Dr Ambedkar reiterated the aim of the struggle and recounted his endeavours for peaceful negotiations. "We will not die if we are not allowed in the Temple, nor are we going to be immortalized by gaining entry. We are fighting for equal rights as human beings, and we are not going to accept anything less," he declared, evoking thunderous applause.

The public meeting was followed by a procession to Kala Ram Temple, led by Dr Ambedkar. Accompanied by a band playing martial tunes and several volunteers, they were joined by a significant turnout of women—a groundbreaking moment as it marked *the first time Untouchable women participated in such a mass movement* [emphasis added]. They were followed by thousands of orderly protesters, marching with discipline and resolve. Upon reaching the temple, they found the gates closed and barricaded, guarded by a contingent of armed police. After a discussion with the Police Superintendent, Dr Ambedkar led the procession to the Godavari River, where another rally took place.

The following day, a peaceful agitation commenced in front of the temple gates. Each of the four gates was heavily guarded by hundreds of armed policemen. The Police Superintendent had set up

---

5 The Kala Ram Temple in Nashik, Maharashtra, was constructed in 1782 at the site believed to have been inhabited by Ram, Sita and Laxman during their exile.

an office in a tent erected directly in front of the temple, anticipating potential nighttime disturbances from the protestors. Instead, the protestors took turns forming a human barricade, effectively sealing off the temple from entry. The agitation continued for several days.

As the end of March 1930 approached, the auspicious occasion of Ram Navami, Lord Ram's birth anniversary, drew near. After being sealed for about a month, the trustees finally reopened the temple. Biding for this moment, the protestors sprang into action, forming a human blockade at the entryway and demanding that worship be allowed on a first-come, first-serve basis. The gates were swiftly closed once more, leading to the arrest of thousands. As the police charged at the demonstrators, they were rounded up and loaded into police vans before being transported to local jails, which soon became overcrowded. They were then taken to the outskirts of the city and left without food, water or shelter. However, they remained undeterred and marched back singing and chanting.

Two days after Ram Navami, tradition dictated a procession of Lord Ram's chariot through Nashik city. Although the Untouchables were not permitted entry into the temple, traditionally, they were allowed to pull the chariot. In light of the ongoing protests, a middle ground was reached: the Upper-Caste Hindus would haul the chariot up to the temple's main gate, after which it would be dragged by the Untouchables.

The priests had announced a specific time for the procession to start, but the Upper-Caste Hindus came together much earlier. They swiftly led the chariot, encouraged by the priests, advancing even beyond the main gate. This caught the protestors off guard, but they quickly mobilized and collectively brought the chariot to a halt midway. As skirmishes broke out, the chariot was diverted from its path. The police intervened, indiscriminately targeting the protestors, including women and children. Riots ensued, leading to the burning of several shops and the destruction of several properties, bicycles and cars in the resulting fire. Many protestors, including Dr Ambedkar, were injured.

The majority of those injured were Untouchables, who were understandably enraged and inclined towards retaliation. However, Dr Ambedkar managed to prevent the crowd from resorting to violence. Gatherings near the temple were now prohibited, and would warrant arrest. The issue was brought before the court, leading to the temporary suspension of the movement pending the court's decision.

During that period, Mahatma Gandhi challenged the salt laws imposed by the British through the *Dandi March* in the town of Dandi, Gujarat. Gandhiji also declared a nationwide Civil Disobedience Movement against British rule on behalf of the Congress Party.[6]

---

6 The parallel between the movements led by Mahatma Gandhi and Dr Ambedkar, respectively, becomes apparent here. Indeed, Dr Ambedkar's declaration of social independence for Untouchables coincided with Mahatma Gandhi's declaration of political independence for India.

PART III

Constitutional Reforms in India: The Two Parallel Tracks

CHAPTER SEVEN

The Government of India Act, 1919 and Southborough Committee

When Lokmanya Bal Gangadhar Tilak was sentenced to a long term of imprisonment in 1908, he remarked in the courtroom: "... In spite of the verdict of the Jury, I still maintain that I am innocent. There are higher powers that rule the destinies of men and nations and I think it may be the will of Providence that the cause I represent may be benefited more by my suffering than by my pen and tongue."[1]

Dr Ambedkar, while not a great believer in divine intervention, emphasized the importance of national unity in the Constituent Assembly in 1946, stating,[2] "... when deciding the destinies of nations, dignities of people, dignities of leaders and dignities of [political] parties ought to count for nothing. The destiny of the country ought to count for everything ... ."

---

1 *Emperor vs B. G. Tilak* (22 July 1908). https://indiankanoon.org/doc/1430706/ (Accessed on 9 January 2021).

2 Constituent Assembly Debates (CAD), Vol. I, (17 December 1946), pp. 99-103, BAWS Vol. 13, pp. 7-27.

Arguably, Dr Ambedkar's entire professional life became inextricably intertwined with Constitutional reforms in India. Indeed, it seems Dr Ambedkar had a tryst with the destiny as far as the formulation of the Indian Constitution was concerned. How else could one explain that Dr Ambedkar was one and the only political leader in India closely involved in every stage of Constitutional Reforms and the Constitution itself, from inception to completion?

A significant milestone in India's Constitutional reforms came in the form of the Government of India Act, 1919. This pivotal legislation was a turning point and emanated from the Montagu-Chelmsford Reforms of 1918. These reforms themselves emerged in response to the persistent demands for self- governance from various Indian political parties. Viceroy Chelmsford summoned the then Secretary of State for India, Edwin Montagu, to explore the feasibility of introducing a system of limited self-government in India.

And, when did the British Government make the historic announcement of the beginning of a new era of "progressive realization of responsible government of a limited character" in India? On 20 August 1917, precisely one day before Dr Ambedkar returned to India (having been compelled to discontinue his advanced studies in England for administrative reasons).

If this isn't a destiny in the making, what else could it be?

To grasp the significance of this monumental Constitutional Reform, a proper perspective is necessary. A useful point of departure for that could be the political evolution of India, spanning from the founding of the Indian National Congress in 1885 to the historic announcement in 1917.

Political Context (1885-1918)

While Dr Ambedkar was studying in the USA and England, India's political climate was going through a metamorphosis. The onset of

World War I in 1914 led to serious conflicts between then prevailing two factions of the Indian National Congress (INC), India's largest and most prominent political organization. The Congress also had major differences with the All-India Muslim League, an organization created to put forward the demands of the Muslims in the national discourse.

The Indian National Congress was founded in December 1885 with an aim to create a platform to voice Indian public opinion.[3] In its initial years, the Congress made modest demands in the arena of civil rights, administrative and economic policies, besides Constitutional reforms, typically through resolutions passed in its Annual Sessions. The Congress leaders subscribing to these means of Petition, Prayer and Protest to exert pressure on the Government came to be known as the Moderates. Prominent Moderate leaders included A.O. Hume, W.C. Banerjee, Surendra Nath Banerjee, Dadabhai Naoroji, Pherozeshah Merwanjee Mehta, Gopal Krishna Gokhale, Badruddin Tyyabji and Justice Mahadev Govind Ranade, among others.

The demands of the INC were mainly political in nature. The Congress had refrained from raising social issues that were pertinent in the context of Indian society. In fact, Dadabhai Naoroji during his 1886 Presidential Address in Calcutta said, "We are met together as a political body to represent to our rulers our political aspirations, not to discuss social reforms."[4]

While this notion was shared by several prominent members, there was a section of the Congress which did not subscribe to this thinking.

---

3 Bipan Chandra, *History of Modern India* (Hyderabad: Orient Blackswan, 2009, Reprint 2018), pp. 169, 199.

4 Johnson Gordon, *Provincial Politics and Indian Nationalism: Bombay and the Indian National Congress 1880-1915* (New York: Cambridge University Press, 1974), p. 35.

Justice Ranade, an eminent Jurist, Historian, Economist, Educationist and one of the tallest social reformers of the 19th century, was very much opposed to the unwillingness of the Congress over taking up sensitive social issues. He argued:[5]

> You cannot have a good social system when you find yourself low in the scale of political rights, nor can you be fit to exercise political rights and privileges unless your social system is based on reason and justice. You cannot have a good economic system when your social arrangements are imperfect. If your religious ideas are low and grovelling you cannot succeed in social, economic and political spheres. This interdependence is not accident but is the law of our nature.

Ranade, along with Raghunath Rao, founded the Indian (National) Social Conference in 1887. The Social Conference virtually became the 'Reform Cell' of the Indian National Congress, and was viewed as an adjunct platform to provide an opportunity to those who were keen to discuss social problems after the business of the Congress was over.[6] The Congress and the Social Conference worked in tandem with each other till 1895. The 1895 Session, however, saw both the organizations coming to conflict with each other, and the relations between them did not remain cordial and cooperative thereafter.

As explained later by Dr Ambedkar:[7]

---

5 C. Yajnesvara Chintamani (ed.), *India Social Reform in Four Parts – Being a Collection of Essays, Addresses and Speeches* (Madras, Thompson & Co., 1901, Reprint 2007), Part-II, pp. 127-28.

6 *The Indian National Congress* (Madras: G. A. Natesan, 1909) p. 111.

7 Dr B. R. Ambedkar, *What Congress and Gandhi Have Done to Untouchables*, BAWS, Vol. 9 (Bombay: Thacker and Co., 1945) .

> In 1895, when the Congress met in Poona ..., this Anti-Social Reform section rebelled and threatened to burn the Congress *pandal* if the Congress allowed it to be used by the Social Conference. This opposition to the Social Conference was headed by no other person than the late Mr Tilak, one of those social Tories and political radicals ....
>
> This rebellion had one effect. It settled that the Congress was not to entertain any question of social reform no matter how urgent. This is the explanation why no Congress President after l895 has referred to the question of social reform in his Presidential Address. The Congress by its action in 1895 had become a purely political body with no interest and no concern in the removal or mitigation of social wrongs.

* * *

Given the limited success achieved by means of Petition, Prayer and Protest of the Congress in its initial years, in the decade of 1890s, a new group emerged within the Party that was critical of the ideology and the methods of the then leadership. This new group came to be known as the Extremists, a contrast to the Moderates. The leaders of the Extremists group included Lala Lajpat Rai, Lokmanya Bal Gangadhar Tilak, Bipin Chandra Pal, Aurobindo Ghose, Rajnarayan Bose, and Ashwini Kumar Dutt.

While the Moderates played a critical role in the functioning of the Congress for nearly two decades (1885-1905), the Extremists started gaining a dominant influence in the functioning of the Congress from 1905.

The Moderates and Extremists were at loggerheads with each other at the Surat Session of the Congress in 1907 which led to a split within the Party.[8] It was around this time that the All-India

8 'Indian National Congress – INC Timeline,' Indian National Congress, accessed June 28, 2020, https://www.inc.in/en/inc-timeline/1905-1915.

Muslim League was formed (30 December 1906). This meant that the nationalistic response against the British Government was going to be divided for the next few years.

When the British decided to take the British Indian Army to fight on the frontiers of World War I, it provoked the first ever, nationwide political debate in India. Voices calling for political independence were getting explicit and louder. The political opportunity of the time made it imperative for different factions to set aside their differences and work together.

Accordingly, the two factions of the INC re-united and came together with the Muslim League towards a common goal in the pivotal Lucknow Session in 1916, with efforts of Bal Gangadhar Tilak and Muhammad Ali Jinnah.[9] The two, along with Mrs Annie Besant, launched a movement to press for Home Rule,[10] or Indian participation in the affairs of their own country. The All India Home Rule League was formed to demand a Dominion Status for India within the British Empire.

* * *

Montagu–Chelmsford Reforms 1918

The British Government made a significant announcement on 20 August 1917, adopting "a policy of increasing association of Indians in every branch of the administration and gradual development of self-governing institutions, with a view to the progressive realization of responsible government in India as an integral part of the British

---

9 https://www.inc.in/en/inc-timeline/1915-1925

10 Bipan Chandra, Mridula Mukherjee, Aditya Mukherjee, et al. *India's Struggle for Independence, 1857-1947* (Penguin Books, 1989).

Empire".[11] The new policy involved far-reaching changes in the administrative, legislative and financial framework of governance. This was the beginning of a new era in India—progressive realization of responsible government of a limited character.

Together, Montagu and Chelmsford formulated and supervised implementation of the so-called Montagu-Chelmsford Reforms (also called Montford Reforms), which gave greater authority to local Indian representative bodies and paved the way towards a free India. The reforms were outlined in the Montagu-Chelmsford Report titled 'Constitutional Reforms in India', which was published on 8 July 1918.

* * *

When the British Government announced the policy regarding "progressive realization of responsible government in India", leading Indian politicians were expecting such a declaration from the British Government and were already formulating schemes for changes in the Constitutional structure of India in anticipation.

A particularly important scheme was the so-called 'The Congress-League Scheme' (also known as the Lucknow Pact).[12] It was a scheme of political reforms supported by both the Congress and the Muslim League. The Scheme had come into existence in 1916, a year before the above-mentioned historic announcement.

The Congress was keen on giving the Congress-League Scheme the status and character of a National Demand. Obviously, this could

---

11 Richard Danzig, 'The Announcement of August 20th, 1917', *The Journal of Asian Studies,* Vol. 28, no. 1 (November 1968), pp. 19-37. https://doi.org/10.2307/2942837 (accessed 28 June 2020).

12 'CAD India'. CAD. https://www.constitutionofindia.net/historical_constitutions/the_congress_league_scheme_1916__inc___aiml__1 January, 1916 (accessed 28 June 2020).

happen only if the Scheme had the backing of all communities in India. Since the Muslim League had already accepted the Scheme, there was no need to secure their backing. Next in numbers came the Depressed Classes. What happened immediately thereafter was most unusual.[13]

In the Annual Session of the Indian National Congress held at Calcutta in December 1917, the Congress passed the resolution:[14] "This Congress urges upon the people of India the necessity, justice and righteousness of removing all disabilities imposed by custom upon the Depressed Classes, the disabilities being of a most vexatious and oppressive character, subjecting those Classes to considerable hardship and inconvenience."

Describing it as a "strange event", many years later, Dr Ambedkar reminded that the Congress had never done such a thing before, although it had functioned for 32 years … . "No Congress President has referred to the question of Social Reform in his Presidential Address since 1898 … . It was even contrary to its declared policy … ."[15] He questioned[16] what made the Congress "take cognizance of the Untouchables? Was it because of a change in its angle of vision or was it because of some ulterior motive?"

According to Dr Ambedkar, the Congress Party was anxious but sceptical about getting the support of the Depressed Classes for the Congress-League Scheme. They, therefore, sought help from Sir Narayan Chandavarkar, who was a former President of the Congress. As the then President of the Depressed Classes Mission Society, he had considerable influence over the Depressed Classes. It was as

13 Ambedkar, *What Congress and Gandhi Have Done to Untouchables*, Vol. 9.

14 *Ibid.*

15 *Ibid.*

16 *Ibid.*

a result of his influence that some of the Depressed Class leaders agreed to give support to the Congress-League Scheme, but on the condition that the Congress passed a resolution for the removal of the social disabilities of the Untouchables.

Explaining this genesis of the Congress Resolution of 1917 on the Depressed Classes, Dr Ambedkar concluded that "there was an ulterior motive behind the Congress Resolution. That motive was not a spiritual motive. It was a political motive".[17]

Three months later, under the auspices of the Depressed Classes Mission Society of India, Karmaveer Vithal Ramji Shinde organized its First All-India Depressed Classes Conference in Bombay (March 1918). In that meeting as well, Sir Chandavarkar appealed to the conscience of the country to remove the blot of Untouchability. Incidentally, while speaking at the Conference, Lokmanya Tilak said, "Untouchability is a disease and it must be removed." Reportedly, Tilak also said, "If God was to tolerate Untouchability, he would not recognize him as God at all."

At the conclusion of the Conference, a manifesto was issued to the effect that they would not observe Untouchability in their everyday affairs. While all prominent leaders signed the declaration, Tilak refrained from signing it,[18] thus confirming Dr Ambedkar calling him a "political radical but a social Tory".

The Government of India Act, 1919

The Montagu-Chelmsford Report formed the basis of the Government of India Act, 1919. The Act received the Royal assent on 23 December 1919. King-Emperor George V issued a Proclamation that clarified the

---

17 Ibid.

18 Keer, Dhananjay, op cit. p. 37.

intent of the Act *vis-a-vis* larger political freedom and Constitutional Reforms for India. The Proclamation *inter alia* stated:

> The Act of 1858 transferred the administration from the Company to the Crown and laid the foundations of public life which exist in India today. The Act of 1861 sowed the seed of representative institutions, and the seed was quickened into life by the Act of 1909. The Act which has now become law entrusts the elected representative of the people with a definite share in the Government and points the way to full responsible Government hereafter.[19]

The salient features of the Government of India Act, 1919 included:

1. An introduction of dyarchy[20] in the Provincial Government
2. Bicameral Central legislature
3. Pronouncement of the Governor as the Executive Head of the Provincial Government
4. Pronouncement of Governor-General as the Chief Executive Authority at the National level, and
5. Provision of three Indian members in the six member Viceroy's Executive Council.

The Act also assured that a Commission would be appointed after 10 years to review the working and progress made under the Act.

The Congress Party was not happy. In a Special Session of the INC at Bombay under the Presidency of Syed Hasan Imam, it

---

19 Joan Nwasike and Dustan Maina (ed.), *Key Principles of Public Sector Reforms: Commonwealth Case Studies* (London: Commonwealth Secretariat, 2018).

20 Dyarchy meant government by two independent authorities as joint heads.

declared the reforms to be "disappointing" and "unsatisfactory"[21] and demanded effective self-government instead. While Tilak termed the Montford reforms as "unworthy and disappointing—a sunless dawn", Annie Besant found them "unworthy of England to offer and India to accept".[22] Gandhiji apparently commented that "the Reforms ... were only a method of further draining India of her wealth and of prolonging her servitude". At the other extreme, Dr Ambedkar referred to the Government of India Act, 1919 as the "British Constitution of India".[23]

Southborough Franchise Committee

As a follow-up action under the Government of India Act, 1919, three committees were set up, i.e., the Franchise Committee, the Function Committee and the Committee on Home Administration.

The Franchise Committee was headed by Lord Southborough and was assigned the task of redefining the electoral franchise within the framework of Constitutional Reform. There were a series of consultations with representatives of different interests and communities, including organizations (or those working) for the Untouchables.

---

21 'Indian National Congress – INC Timeline', Indian National Congress, accessed June 28, 2020, https://www.inc.in/en/inc-timeline/1915-1925.

22 G.S. Chhabra, *Advance Study in the History of Modern India* (Vol.3: *1920-1947)*, (Delhi: Lotus Press, 2007), p. 2.

23 Centre for Law and Policy Research. 2017. 'The Congress League Scheme 1916'. Constituent Assembly Debates. https://www.constitutionofindia.net/historical_constitutions/the_congress_league_scheme_1916__inc___aiml__1st January 1916 (accessed 24 May 2020).

Dr Ambedkar's academic credentials had come to the attention of the British who invited him to testify before the Southborough Committee along with the then leaders of Untouchables.

Dr Ambedkar gave his testimony before the Southborough Committee on 27 January 1919 and subsequently also submitted a Supplementary Written Note.

This was Dr Ambedkar's first foray into public life, a journey that would continue for the rest of his life. Nobody could have imagined at that time that this issue of franchise was going to bring Dr Ambedkar into direct conflict with Mahatma Gandhi 13 years later, with Dr Ambedkar becoming the only politician whom Mahatma Gandhi contested by resorting to a "fast unto death"!

* * *

Evidence before the Southborough Committee[24]

In his testimony before the Southborough Committee (27 January 1919), Dr Ambedkar focused on two issues:

(1) The definition of the franchise was unfavourable to Untouchables; it did not allow them to vote in large numbers thereby preventing them from becoming a notable political force. He, therefore, suggested lowering the bar so as to enable greater participation of Untouchables in the political process.

(2) As to the choice between the electoral systems, Dr Ambedkar recommended, "either to reserve seats for those minorities that cannot otherwise secure personal representation or grant communal electorates." (He changed his position almost immediately, as discussed below).

24 For a fuller summary, see Jadhav, Narendra, *Ambedkar Writes*, (2014), Vol. I, pp 17-35.

Around the same time, Dr Ambedkar wrote a letter to *The Times of India* (16 January 1919) under a pseudonym (he could not write under his own as he was a Professor in a Government college in Bombay). In the letter, Dr Ambedkar argued that Home Rule was as much the birth right of an Untouchable, as it was of a Brahmin. Accordingly, the first duty of the advanced classes was to educate, enlighten and elevate the Depressed Classes.[25]

In the Supplementary Written Statement, submitted to the Southborough Committee (27 January 1919), however, Dr Ambedkar came out *unambiguously in favour of "Communal Electorates"* instead of the "Reserved Seats" formula [emphasis added].

Dr Ambedkar argued that the Indian society is ridden into caste and religious communities. As such, any scheme of franchise must be representative of opinions as well as persons.

Dr Ambedkar argued:

> Territorial constituencies ... fail to secure personal representation to members of minor groups. The 'Touchable' Hindus, Muslims, Parsis, etc., have on a secular plane common material interests. There will be in such groups landlords, labourers and capitalists. The Untouchables are, however, isolated by the Hindus from any kind of social participation. They have been dehumanized by socio-religious disabilities almost to the status of slaves. They are denied the universally accepted rights of citizenship. Their interests are distinctively their own interests and none else can truly voice them ... .

About the issue of definition of the franchise, Dr Ambedkar emphasised: "At present, when all the avenues of acquiring wealth are closed, it is unwise to require from the Untouchables a high property qualification. To deny them the opportunities of acquiring

---

25 As quoted in Keer, Dhananjay, *op cit,* p. 40.

wealth and then ask from them a property qualification (for voting) is to add insult to injury."

Dr Ambedkar suggested that the franchise should be pitched so low that it would enable the Untouchables, as many as possible, to educate into political life because they 'are too degraded to be conscious of themselves'.

He also recommended that the Untouchables of the Bombay Presidency be allowed to elect nine members of which, one member elected from among themselves, should be representing the Untouchables in the Central Legislative Council.

Dr Ambedkar severely criticized the Congress Scheme which offered communal representation only to the Muslims and left Untouchables to seek representation in general electorate. He maintained: "To educate the Untouchables ... into pro-Touchable, and the Touchable into anti-Untouchable, and then to propose that the two should fight out at an open poll is to betray signs of mental aberration or a mentality fed on cunning. But it never be forgotten that the Congress is largely composed of men who are by design political Radicals and social Tories ... ."

Dr Ambedkar emphatically argued that the communal representation with reserved seats for the Untouchables will not perpetuate the social divisions. In fact, they could "act as a potent solvent for dissolving them by providing opportunities for contact, co-operation and re-socialization of fossilized attitudes ...".

Dr Ambedkar noted sharply that if the so-called Upper Caste Hindus are insisting on application of the principle of self-determination in India as a whole, it would be "patently wrong if the same principle was *not* applied to the Untouchables as well". Dr Ambedkar forcefully put across the view that communal representation cannot be withheld from the Untouchables because "communal representation and self-determination are nothing but two different phrases which express the same notion".

* * *

With this eloquent pitch for unalienable (natural) rights in a 'responsible government', the inherently republican stance of Dr Ambedkar became clearly evident. And, this was only a beginning —his first foray into Republicanism, as the basis for Constitutional Reforms in India.

CHAPTER EIGHT

Simon Commission, 1928 and Constitutional Reforms

As discussed in the last chapter, the Government of India Act, 1919 had brought in a system of dyarchy for governing the Provinces of British India. This was the first major step in the process of progressive realization of responsible government in India as an integral part of the British Empire. The political context was changing.

Political Context (1919-1928)

Within a year after the Government of India Act, 1919, was passed, the first-ever General Elections in British India were to be held for electing the members to the Imperial Legislative Council and the Provincial Councils. The Imperial Legislative Council comprised the new Central Legislative Assembly and the Council of State. The Central Legislative Council consisted of 104 seats of which 66 were contested while the Council of State consisted of 34 seats of which 24 were contested. The Provincial Councils, in aggregate, consisted of 637 seats of which 440 were contested.[1]

---

1 'New Indian Councils: Failure of Boycott Movement', *The Times*, 8 January 1921, Issue 42613, p. 9.

The response of the Indian political community to the Government of India Act, 1919, was lukewarm, at best. The Congress decided not to contest the General Elections of 1920. In fact, Mahatma Gandhi gave a call for a boycott of the election. However, the call did not find enough takers.[2] The Parliament was inaugurated on 9 February 1921.[3]

After the demise of Lokmanya Tilak in 1920, Gandhiji effectively took over the leadership of the Congress and led the nation through the Non-Cooperation Movement against the oppressive policies of the British Government of India, specifically Rowlatt Act[4] and the Jallianwala Bagh Massacre (13 April 1919). The movement was perhaps the first-ever countrywide mass mobilization for *Satyagraha*. It, however, ended abruptly in 1922 when Gandhiji was sent to jail in March 1922 (to early 1924), and tried for sedition.

During this time, the Congress was divided into two camps—*Swarajists* who advocated Council entry (through election) and No-changers who advocated constructive work.[5]

The Second General Elections for both the Central Legislative Assembly and Provincial Assemblies were held in November 1923. The Central Legislative Assembly had 145 seats, of which 105 were elected by the public.[6] The *Swaraj* Party fought the elections and achieved considerable success.

---

2 Ibid.

3 'New Era For India: Delhi Parliament Opened, King's Messages', *The Times*, 10 February 1921, Issue 42641, p. 10.

4 The Anarchical and Revolutionary Crimes Act of 1919, also known as Black Act, gave the British Government the power to arrest any person without trial.

5 Bipin Chandra, Mridula Mukherjee, Aditya Mukherjee, et al., *India's Struggle for Independence, 1857-1947* (Penguin Books, 1989) pp. 223-24.

6 'Indian Election Results: Strength of Extremists', *The Times*, 15 December 1923, Issue 43525, p. 11.

When Gandhiji was released from jail in 1924, he was elected as President of the Congress Party. Despite his efforts to reconcile the factions, he initially found only moderate success. However, the *Swaraj* Party suffered a major setback with the death of Chittaranjan Das in 1925. This was reflected in their lacklustre performance in the Third General Elections of 1926, compelling their leaders to return to the Congress fold.

* * *

In the meantime, the Indian political spectrum had widened with the entry of several parties and players with varied priorities. In addition to the *Swarajists* and the No-changers, there was also a faction of Congress, particularly among the younger cadre, that was sympathetic to the cause of socialism.

The other prominent political force, the Muslim League, had a brief history of working closely with the INC during the Khilafat Movement[7] after World War I. However, in the subsequent years, differences cropped up between the two parties, its leaders and ideologies. Muhammad Shafi, M.A. Jinnah and Sir Muhammad Iqbal were the frontline leaders of the League in the 1920s.

Some other political currents that also emerged comprised the spread of Marxism (the Communist Party of India was formed in 1920), growth of trade unionism (All India Trade Union Congress—AITUC—was formed in 1920),[8] and Anti-Caste movements

---

7 A pan-Islamic political protest campaign (1919-1924) launched by Sunni Muslims of British India against the sanctions imposed on the Caliph of the Ottoman Caliphate after the World War I.

8 The 1920s saw the labour movement in India getting strengthened by the Communist-led trade unions. Several calls for strike were given by textile workers in 1924, 1925, 1928 and 1929. Reportedly, the April 1929 strike covered as many as 75,000 workers from textile mills in Bombay.

(prominent one included 'Self-Respect Movement' in 1925 under 'Periyar' E.V. Ramasamy Naicker in Madras).

Around this time, Dr Ambedkar made a formal entry into public life. As indicated in Chapter 4, he had established a social organization called *Bahishkrit Hitakarini Sabha* (9 March 1924). On behalf of this social organization, Dr Ambedkar was trying to persuade the British Government to increase the number of Nominated Members representing the Depressed Classes in the Bombay Province. In December 1925, the British Government finally raised the number from one to two and appointed Dr Ambedkar and Dr P.G. Solanki to those positions. For Dr Ambedkar, this was going to be the beginning of a long and distinguished career as a Legislator.

Appointment of the Simon Commission

The Government of India Act of 1919 mandated the appointment of a Commission after 10 years to review the progress of the Governance Scheme and propose further reforms. However, in 1927, fearing potential electoral defeat by the Labour Party, the Conservative Government in Britain appointed a seven-member Indian Statutory Commission, known as the Simon Commission, to assess Indian Constitutional Reforms. Lord Birkenhead, the Secretary of State for India at that time, oversaw the formation of the Commission,[9] with Sir John Simon serving as Chairman (the Commission was named after him), along with Clement Attlee (who later became the Prime Minister), and five other British Members of Parliament.

When the Simon Commission arrived in India in 1928 to evaluate the state of Indian Constitutional Reforms, widespread outrage erupted throughout the country. This was primarily due to the

9 C.F. Andrews, *Routledge Revivals: India and the Simon Report (1930)* (London: Routledge, 1930) p. 31, https://doi.org/10.4324/9781315445007

Commission's lack of Indian representation, despite its mandate to shape India's future. Leaders from every political faction argued vehemently that Indian participation was essential in determining the country's political destiny.

During its Annual Session in 1927 held at Madras, the INC decided to boycott the Simon Commission "at every stage and in every form".[10] The INC also convened an All Parties Conference to draft a Constitution for India, a move supported by most political parties. However, within the Muslim League leadership, there was a disagreement on the issue. Ultimately, Mohammad Ali Jinnah carried the majority with him in favour of boycotting the Commission.

The widespread outrage led to *hartals*, mass rallies, processions and black-flag demonstrations in major Indian cities.[11] The Commission was met with the slogan of "Simon, Go Back" across the country. In Lahore, clashes between protestors and police resulted in injuries to senior Congress leader Lala Lajpat Rai. He succumbed to these injuries a few weeks later. Gandhiji wrote in *Young India* that the best tribute for Lala Lajpat Rai would be to "work for *Swaraj* and all it implies with redoubled zeal".[12]

* * *

Amid widespread opposition to Simon Commission, the British Government had apparently challenged Indians to prove their capability in drafting a Constitution of India. Earlier, in 1925, Lord Birkenhead, the Secretary of State for India, had reportedly issued

---

10 'Indian National Congress – INC Timeline', Indian National Congress, accessed June 28, 2020, https://www.inc.in/en/inc-timeline/1925-1935.

11 Bipan Chandra, Mridula Mukherjee, et al., *India's Struggle for Independence*, p. 252.

12 Ibid, p. 252.

a similar challenge in the House of Lords. The INC at its Annual Session in Madras (1927) accepted this challenge.

After an all-party-meeting in February and May 1928, the Congress formed a Committee chaired by Motilal Nehru to draft a *Swaraj* Constitution of India—supposedly the first *Indian* attempt at Constitution-making.[13] The Committee included members such as Tej Bahadur Sapru, Subhas Chandra Bose, Madhav Shrihari Aney, Mangal Singh, Shuab Qureshi, Ali Imam and G.R. Pradhan, with Jawaharlal Nehru serving as the Committee's Secretary. The Motilal Nehru-led Committee finalized its report in August 1928, which is elaborated upon in Chapter 9.

Dr Ambedkar, a nominated member of the Bombay Legislative Council at that time, was elected to serve on the Bombay Province Committee for Cooperation with the Simon Commission. He testified before this Committee.

Dr Ambedkar's Response to the Simon Commission

While the Congress, Muslim League and most other political parties boycotted the Simon Commission, Dr Ambedkar on the other hand, submitted a Statement detailing safeguards for protection of the interests of the Depressed Classes. The Statement was submitted to the Simon Commission on 29 May 1928, on behalf of his social organization i.e., *Bahishkrita Hitakarini Sabha.* This important Statement was hailed by Dr Ambedkar's supporters as a 'Manifesto of Untouchables' Rights', while many others dubbed him as a "British stooge and a traitor".[14]

---

13 Strictly speaking, this is not true. There were atleast two attempts earlier, which have been discussed in detail in Chapter 9.

14 Keer, Dr Ambedkar, op cit. p 116

In his Statement, at the outset, Dr Ambedkar explained the reason why his organization did not agitate (like other political and social organizations). He said: "... those in charge of the affairs from the Viceroy downwards have cultivated the habit of recognizing the noisy few and forgetting the dumb millions ..."[15]

Dr Ambedkar's Statement is divided into two parts: first, 'Protection through Adequate Representation' and second, 'Protection through Guarantees'.

As far as adequate representation to the Depressed Classes is concerned, Dr Ambedkar argued as follows:

1. Promises made in the Montagu-Chelmsford Report "were thrown to the wind by the Southborough Committee".
2. The Depressed Classes should have 22 representatives in a Council composed of 140 members.
3. The Southborough Committee grossly underestimated the numerical strength of the Depressed Classes in Bombay Presidency. Quoting the Director of the Census of India 1921, it was pointed out that their number ought to be placed between 55 to 60 million in India, and around 10.8 per cent of the population of the Bombay Presidency. "On the basis of their strength alone, the Depressed Classes are entitled to 15 seats out of a total of 140 ... ."
4. Those communities which have limited power to protect themselves in the social struggle (due to low educational and economic status) should have greater electoral advantage than the rest. No other community is "burdened with ... grave disabilities which form the common lot of the Depressed Classes".

15 For summary see Jadhav: *Ambedkar Writes,* 2014 Vol. I, pp. 36-50.

5. The British Government has been overly generous to the Mohammedans because of the "distinction" made on the basis of the "political importance of the different communities". "This invidious distinction is at the root of all the communal troubles and is destructive of the principle of equal opportunity".
6. From the standpoint of political education, the principle of "election" is decidedly better than that of "nomination". Usually, two objections are raised against the application of the principle of election to the Depressed Classes:
   a.) Difficulty in forming constituencies, and
   b.) Difficulty in getting a sufficiently large electorate.

The first objection is invalid because the Muslims and the Europeans are "not less scattered than the Depressed Classes" and yet forming constituencies for them does not come in the way.

The second objection is entirely valid given the "exiting pitch of the franchise" which is "unjustifiable on every ground".

> It has turned a responsible Government into a mockery. It means *a Government of the whole (Bombay) Presidency of two crores of people by a minority of seven lakhs who happen to have the good fortune of being voters under the existing franchise* [emphasis added]. Such a state of things is clearly vicious and cannot be allowed to continue in future, if there is to be a responsible Government, not merely in name but also in fact ...

In the Statement, Dr Ambedkar lamented that the question of franchise occupies in Congress politics a very subordinate place as compared to the question of the transfer of powers. According to him, the question of the franchise is so vital that "upon its determination alone can depend, the degree of the transfer of political power ... ."

> In the way in which [the franchise] is determined at present … the principal aim of representative government has been lost sight of altogether. *Franchise means the right to determine the terms of associated life* … the very exigencies of representative government demand that the franchise … must be fixed so low as to bring it within the reach of the large majority of the poor and the oppressed sections of society. *Indeed adult franchise*[16] *is the only system of franchise which can be in keeping with the true meaning of that term* [emphasis added] …

Regarding the apprehension that a lowering of the franchise "will result in the inclusion of a significant portion of unintelligent people", Dr Ambedkar points out:

> Large property is not incompatible with ignorance. Nor is abject poverty incompatible with high degree of intelligence. Property may as well dull the edge of intelligence. Consequently, *the adherence of the Government to a high property qualification as an insurance against ignorance is nothing but a superstition, which is sedulously cultivated by the Classes and fostered by the Government in order to deprive the masses of their right to the making of their Government [emphasis added].*
>
> Free elections in general constituencies are out of the question as far as the Depressed Classes are concerned.... 'it would be sufficient if the Depressed Classes are provided with reserved seats in the general constituencies'.[17]

---

16 It is most remarkable that Dr Ambedkar was talking about universal adult franchise at a time when Europe was still considering female franchise and the US, the vote for African Americans. See Raja Sekhar Vundru, 'The Other Father', *Outlook* (Special Issue), 20 August 2012.

17 In all, 18 Depressed Class Associations submitted their Memoranda. Interestingly, 16 out of these 18 associations pleaded for "separate

> The right of the Depressed Classes to be represented in the (Central) Legislative Assembly has not been recognized in 1919. Three members from the Depressed Classes of the Bombay Presidency should be elected to the (Central) Legislative Assembly.

As far as the protection for Depressed Classes through guarantees is concerned, Dr Ambedkar in his Statement demanded the inclusion of clauses in the Constitution, as its fundamental part, relating to guarantees of the civil rights for the Depressed Classes as a minority. The guarantees proposed, included:

- earmarking an equitable and just proportion of the total grant for education for the benefit of the Depressed Classes,
- the right of unrestricted recruitment in the army, navy and the police without any limitation on the grounds of the Caste,
- priority in the matter of recruitment to all posts, gazetted as well as non-gazetted, in all civil services,
- appointment of a special inspector of police ... for every district, from amongst the Depressed Classes,
- the right of the Depressed Classes to effective representation ... on the Local Bodies, and,
- the right of the Depressed Classes to appeal to the Government of India in cases of violation of these rights by the Provincial Government.

In conclusion, the Statement clarifies:

---

electorates" for the Depressed Classes. Dr Ambedkar also subsequently changed his position and championed the cause of "separate electorates", leading to Gandhi-Ambedkar conflict in the Second Round Table Conference as discussed in Chapter 10.

> Many people in the world have fallen low by force of circumstances. But having fallen they are free to rise. The Depressed Classes, on the other hand, form a solitary case of a people who have remained fallen because their rise is opposed to the religious notions of the majority of their countrymen .... .
>
> So rigorous is the enforcement of the Social Code against the Depressed Classes that any attempt on the part of the Depressed Classes to exercise their elementary rights of citizenship only ends in provoking the majority, to practice the worst form of social tyranny known to history .... .
>
> Nothing can allay ... fears, as the system of guarantees can do. Government is based upon faith and not upon reason. If the Depressed Classes can have no faith in the new Constitution, it is statesmanship to buy that faith if it can be done so with the concession of guarantees herein demanded.

Recommendations by Simon Commission

The Simon Commission submitted a two-volume Report in May 1930. The prominent suggestions in the Report included the abolition of dyarchy and the establishment of autonomous representative governments in the Provinces. The other key recommendations of the Report included the Governor having administrative powers to protect the different communities and discretionary powers in relation to internal security; increase in the number of members of Provincial Legislative Council; the Governor-General having total power to appoint the members of the Cabinet; and the Government of India having complete control over the High Court.

The Simon Commission Report also recommended that separate Communal electorates be retained (and extended to other communities) but only until tensions between the Hindus and Muslims had died down. There was to be no provision for universal franchise. The idea of Federalism was acknowledged and appreciated. However, it would not be implemented in near future. It also suggested that the Indian Army should be Indianised, though British forces must be retained.

The Simon Commission in its Report also recommended 10 reserved seats for the Depressed Classes in joint electorates (and 33 per cent of elected seats out of 140 seats to the Muslims with separate electorates).

In the absence of participation by the Indian National Congress, however, the Report remained ineffectual and defunct. In order to break the impasse, the British Government had to resort to another set of consultations, which came to be known as the Round Table Conference (RTC).

CHAPTER NINE

Swaraj Constitutional Reforms: From Tilak to Motilal Nehru (1895-1928)

The British Constitutional Reforms in India began in 1919 with the Southborough Committee, which emanated from the Montagu-Chelmsford Reforms, 1918 and the Government of India Act, 1919 (as discussed in Chapter 7).

Since the establishment of the Congress Party in 1885 and amid growing Indian aspirations for "self-government", concurrent efforts towards Constitutional Reforms aimed at achieving "*Swaraj*" were underway. Noteworthy among these efforts were:

- *Swaraj* Bill of 1895
- Commonwealth of India Bill of 1925, and
- Motilal Nehru Report of 1928

At this stage, it is informative to examine this "unofficial" evolution of the Constitution of India,[1] which unfolded alongside the British Constitutional Reforms in India.

---

1 Dr Ambedkar had his own version of "unofficial" Constitution, which he had prepared before his election as the Chairman of the Drafting

Swaraj Bill of 1895

The *Swaraj* Bill of 1895, initially championed by Lokmanya Tilak and later dubbed the Home Rule Bill by Annie Besant, is perhaps "the first articulation of a Constitutional imagination by Indians".[2] This visionary bill outlined the initial Constitutional framework for India, comprising 110 articles in a legal format.[3] It proposed dividing the Constitution into four powers: (a) Sovereign (b) Legislative (c) Judicial and (d) Executive (Article 8). All these powers were to be vested in the Parliament of India (Article 10).

Furthermore, the proposed Constitution laid down a number of citizen rights, including Freedom of Expression (Article 17), Right to Property (Article 24), Equality before Law (Article 21) and (curiously) Right to Bear Arms (Article 15). The Constitution also stipulated imprisonment only by competent authority (Article 19) and interestingly, compulsory Primary Education (Article 26) as well as free State Education (Article 25).

Commonwealth of India Bill of 1925

The Commonwealth of India Bill of 1925 originated from the initial drafting efforts of the 'National Convention', chaired by Tej Bahadur

---

Committee of the Indian Constitution. That is extensively discussed in Chapter 15. Moreover, there was yet another attempt to formulate a *Swaraj* Constitution of India i.e. the Sapru Committee Report (1945), which focused on the "Communal Question". However, the Sapru Committee Report received scant attention, with the Muslim League expressing hostility towards it and the Congress showing lukewarm interest.

2 Rohit De's chapter on 'Constitutional Antecedents' in *The Oxford Handbook of the Indian Constitution,* edited by Sujit Choudhary, Madhav Khosla and Pratap Bhanu Mehta, (UK: Oxford University Press, 2016).

3 https://www.constitution of india.net

Sapru in April 1924.[4] Later, in December 1924, an amended version of the Bill was submitted to a Sub-Committee appointed by the so-called All Parties Conference of 1925, presided over by Ms Annie Besant. The Sub-Committee proposed several amendments and then the Bill was finalized by the National Convention in April 1925.[5]

The Commonwealth of India Bill of 1925 resembled a full-fledged Constitution, consisting of 127 Articles organized into 10 chapters. Notably, it featured a section on Fundamental Rights which included, *inter alia*, Freedom of Expression, Gender Equality, Non-discrimination and the Right to Elementary Education, similar to the provisions found in its predecessor, the *Swaraj* Bill of 1895. However, most of these "Fundamental Rights" were subject to restrictions. The Bill also proposed limitations on the franchise by outlining qualifications based on income, land ownership, literacy and education.

Presented in the British Parliament by a leader of the Labour Party in December 1925, the Bill failed to pass due to the Labour Party's defeat in the elections. Nevertheless, the Bill turned out to be an important precursor to the next major attempt at formulating a non-official Constitution of India – i.e., the Motilal Nehru Report.

Motilal Nehru Report of 1928

As described in Chapter 8, the establishment of the Simon Commission in 1927 provoked dissatisfaction among leaders of the nationalist movement due to its lack of Indian representation. In response, the British Government appeared to challenge the Indians, daring them to demonstrate their ability to formulate a Constitution for India independently. In 1925, Lord Birkenhead, then Secretary

---

4 Ibid.

5 National Convention comprised 256 members, mostly legislators and ex-legislators.

of State for India, had reportedly issued a similar challenge in the House of Lords.

In response, the Congress Party at its Annual Session at Madras in December 1927 accepted the challenge and resolved that the Congress Working Committee be empowered to set up a Committee to draft a *Swaraj* Constitution for India.

In May 1928, the said Committee was set up under the Chairmanship of Motilal Nehru with Jawaharlal Nehru as the Secretary. Members of the Committee included, among others, Subhas Chandra Bose and Tej Bahadur Sapru. The report of the Committee, submitted on 10 August 1928 has been referred to as Motilal Nehru Report.

The Motilal Nehru Report (1928) essentially proposed:

(i) A Dominion Status of complete internal self-government for India,

(ii) A Federal setup of government,

(iii) Elections under universal suffrage, and

(iv) A Bill of Rights ('Fundamental Rights').

Salient features of this important document may be summarized as under:

- All powers of the Government and all authority thereof—i.e. Legislative, Executive and Judicial—to be derived from the people.
- There should be a Federal Government with residuary powers vested in the Central Government.
- A Supreme Court should be created.
- The Provinces should be linguistically determined.

- There shall be a Bill of Rights which aims at securing the Fundamental Rights denied to the Indian people.
- There shall be no State religion and women shall have equal rights as citizens.
- There is no provision for separate electorates for *any* community or weightage for minorities. The Report, however, did allow for the reservation of minority seats in Provinces having minorities of at least 10 per cent but that was to be in strict proportion to the size of the community.[6]

The Report elicited a mixed reaction. Politically, the Muslim League rejected it outright. In fact, in 1929, Mohammad Ali Jinnah formulated his "Fourteen Points" which become the core demands of the Muslim community as the *quid pro quo* for participating in an Independent United India.[7]

Several constitutional experts hailed the Motilal Nehru Report. Granville Austin, an American historian and Constitutional expert, pointed out that the Fundamental Rights included in the Motilal Nehru Report were "a close precursor of the Fundamental Rights of the (final) Constitution of India ... 10 out of the 19 sub-clauses re-appear, materially unchanged, and three of the Nehru rights are included in the Directive Principles".[8] Actually, this praise seems to be somewhat misplaced. It can easily be verified that several of these Fundamental Rights were borrowed, word for word, from the Commonwealth of India Bill of 1925 and some even from *Swaraj* Bill of 1895.

---

6 Centre for Law and Policy Research, 'Nehru Report', CADIndia, clpr.org.in, (accessed on 7 May 2020).

7 There were two main objections: Rejection of the Lucknow Pact of 1916 and giving residuary powers to the Centre.

8 Granville Austin, *The Indian Constitution: Cornerstone of a Nation* (Oxford: Clarendon Press, 1966).

Dr Ambedkar was highly critical of the Motilal Nehru Report on the following grounds:

1. While the Nehru Committee consulted all minorities, they did not consult the Depressed Class groups. In fact, the Report stated: "We have not made any special provision for the representation of the Depressed Classes in the Legislatures by way of special electorates or by nomination." The Committee categorically stated that they would not extend either principle.
2. While Motilal Nehru Committee had listed a set of Fundamental Rights, Dr Ambedkar argued:[9]

   > No declaration of rights – however comprehensive in its scope and however clear in its terms and tenor – can ensure the enjoyment of those rights. The guarantee of a right consists not in its declaration but in the provision of a remedy for its enforcement in case it is violated.
   >
   > The Motilal Nehru Committee's Report does not even have an appeal clause against the infringement of the Fundamental Rights. The guarantee in the Nehru Constitution is, therefore, quite illusory.

Some scholars, especially Christophe Jaffrelot and Vidhu Verma, have raised an interesting question. The Motilal Nehru Committee Report was inspired by the Western liberal values such as the notion of a nation as a collection of individuals, not very different from Dr Ambedkar's own line of thinking. Why is then Dr Ambedkar so strongly opposed to the Motilal Nehru Committee? The reason is

---

9 Presidential Address at the All India Depressed Classes Congress in Nagpur (8-9 August 1930). For full text of the Address, see Narendra Jadhav (ed.), *Ambedkar Speaks,* Vol. I. (Delhi: Konark Publishers, 2013), pp. 59-81.

that, despite the yearning "for the emergence of an individualistic society, free from the caste cleavages", Dr Ambedkar recognized that in the hierarchical Indian society, "social equality could be promoted only by relying upon the logic of groups. Untouchables needed to be helped collectively for an unspecified period of transition".[10]

It is generally conceded that despite the merit, the Motilal Committee Report "had little practical result",[11] and the Government of India Act, 1935 owes much to the Simon Commission Report and little, if anything, to the Motilal Nehru Report.

---

10 Refer Jaffrelot (2005), *op cit*, p.56 for this argument.

11 R. Coupland, The Indian Problem: *Report on the Constitutional Problem in India* (New York: Oxford University Press, 1944). www.questia.com (accessed on 6 May 2020).

CHAPTER TEN

Round Table Conferences (1930-32)

Aftermath of Simon Commission

In the backdrop of protests across the country against the Simon Commission, the Congress was hoping to turn the discontent into a popular political struggle. In this regard, a momentum started gathering at the Annual Session of the Congress held at Calcutta in 1928. The Calcutta Session was presided over by Motilal Nehru, the chief architect of the Nehru Report.

The Nehru Report was challenged even within the Congress Party. A section of Congress leaders, mostly comprising the young and radical nationalists, objected to the Nehru Report for acceptance of the Dominion Status as the basis for the future Constitution of India. Interestingly, this camp was led by Jawaharlal Nehru, son of Motilal Nehru, who served as the Secretary of the Motilal Nehru Committee. The camp forcefully advocated acceptance of *Purna Swaraj,* or complete Independence, as the goal of the Congress Party.

While Gandhiji, Motilal Nehru and some others were in favour of giving the British Government of India some time to act on the Nehru Report, under pressure from the younger nationalist leaders, it was decided in the Session that if the British Government of India did not accept a Constitution based on the Dominion Status by the end of one year, the Congress will announce that complete Independence was its goal. The resolution also warned the British Government of India that the Congress Party will resort to a Civil Disobedience Movement to attain its goal.

Meanwhile, the political climate in Britain had undergone a change of regime. In the General Elections in Britain (May 1929), the incumbent Conservative Government lost its majority, which paved the way for the Labour Party to form the Government. Ramsay MacDonald became the Prime Minister of Britain. Shortly thereafter, in October 1929, Viceroy Irwin made a statement regarding the status of India in the British Empire (the Irwin Declaration) which stated: "… I am authorised on behalf of his Majesty's Government to state clearly that in their judgement it is implicit in the Declaration of 1917 that the natural issue of India's Constitutional progress as there contemplated is the attainment of Dominion status."[1]

While the Declaration indicated the eventual attainment of the Dominion Status for India, there was no mention of any timeline. Clearly, this did not go down well with the Congress Party. The Irwin Declaration was going to be the central theme in the Annual Session of Congress scheduled to happen later that year.

Quest for *Purna Swaraj*

In the Lahore Session (December 1929), the Congress decided to pass the *Purna Swaraj* resolution that called for complete Independence

---

1 Centre for Law and Policy Research. 2017. 'Irwin Declaration, 1929'. Constituent Assembly Debates. https://www.constitutionofindia.net/historical_constitutions/irwin_declaration__lord_irwin__1929__31st%20October%201929 (accessed on 24 May 2020).

from the British.[2] A flag of India was hoisted by Jawaharlal Nehru, the elected President of the Congress, on 31 December 1929 and a pledge was read out, which included a readiness to withhold taxes. It was also decided to observe 26 January as Independence Day.

The resolution was a short, 750-word document, and read more like a manifesto. The resolution rationalized the demand for complete Independence on account of the injustice inflicted upon the Indians by the British *Raj*, stating: "The British Government in India has not only deprived the Indian people of their freedom but has based itself on the exploitation of the masses, and has ruined India economically, politically, culturally and spiritually ... . Therefore ... India must sever the British connection and attain *Purna Swaraj* or complete Independence."[3]

The Declaration of Independence was officially promulgated on 26 January 1930. The Indian National Congress, under the stewardship of Gandhiji and other leaders, began to plan a massive non-violent Civil Disobedience Movement. Gandhiji himself, in person, started the movement with the 'Salt Satyagraha' protest march on 12 March 1930 from his ashram in Ahmedabad to Dandi village in Gujarat (hence, also called the Dandi March).

The march covered around 384 km over a span of 24 days, at the end of which Gandhiji picked up grains of salt as a symbol of protest against the salt tax. This action triggered an unprecedented

---

2 'Indian National Congress – INC Timeline', Indian National Congress, https://www.inc.in/en/inc-timeline/1925-1935 (accessed on 28 June 2020).

3 Centre for Law and Policy Research. 2017. 'Declaration of Purna Swaraj', Indian National Congress in 1930. Constituent Assembly Debates. https://www.constitutionofindia.net/historical_constitutions/declaration_of_purna_swaraj__indian_national_congress__1930__26th%20January%201930 (accessed on 24 May 2020).

nationwide response to the Civil Disobedience Movement. Millions of Indians sprang into action by resorting to non-violent protests and non-cooperation with the British *Raj*. British cloth and goods were boycotted and people refused to pay taxes. As many as 60,000 Indians were jailed as a result of the *Salt Satyagraha*. Gandhiji was arrested on the midnight of 4–5 May 1930, and the Congress Working Committee was declared illegal in June. Gandhiji remained in jail for almost a year.

The Congress Party's call for Independence against the British Government failed to garner support from the Muslim League, which opted to abstain from the Civil Disobedience Movement. Earlier, the Muslim League had rejected the Nehru Report, citing reasons such as the Report's neglect of the demand for separate electorates for Muslims, inadequate representation for Muslims, the establishment of *Devanagari* as the official writing system, and the proposal for India to become a *de facto* Unitary State with residuary powers resting at the Centre. Jinnah expressed a "parting of the ways" when his several requests for amendments to the proposal were denied outright, and relations between the Congress and the Muslim League began to sour.[4]

In the March 1929 session of the Muslim League, Jinnah consolidated all 14 demands that had been put forward by the Muslim League during the preparation of the Nehru Report. These demands became known as the 'Fourteen Points of Jinnah'. They included proposals for a Federal Constitution with residuary powers vested in the provinces, a uniform measure of autonomy guaranteed to all provinces, at least one-third representation of Muslims in the Central Legislature, and full religious liberty, among others. These

4 Holt, P. M.; Lambton, Ann K. S.; Lewis, Bernard (1977). *The Cambridge History of Islam*. Cambridge University Press. p. 103ff.

demands significantly shaped the Muslim League's strategy in the ensuing years.

Barely a year later, in the subsequent session of the Muslim League convened on 29 December 1930, Sir Muhammad Iqbal delivered a very important presidential address that would play a crucial role in determining the future of the Hindu-Muslim identity. Sir Iqbal proposed the "formation of a self-governed consolidated North-West Indian Muslim State", whether within or outside the framework of the British Empire.[5]

Historians contend that Iqbal's intent was not to advocate for the Partition of India, but rather for a Federation of autonomous States within India.[6] However, these demands further widened the gulf between the Congress and the League, making any potential compromise appear like a distant dream.

The 1920s witnessed the rise of several revolutionary movements in India, including the Hindustan Socialist Republican Association (HSRA) and Indian Republican Army. The 1920s and early 1930s were marked by both panic and repression on the part of the British authorities in response to these revolutionaries. The execution of Bhagat Singh, Rajguru and Sukhdev in 1931 underscored this crackdown. These developments played a pivotal role in galvanizing national consciousness and resistance against British Rule.

Against the background of this political turbulence, the Fourth General Elections for British India in 1930. These elections were marred by public apathy and were boycotted by major political parties in the country. Nevertheless, the newly elected Central Legislative Assembly started functioning from January 1931.

---

5 Abdur-Rahman Tariq (ed.), *Speeches and Statements of Iqbal* (Lahore: Sh. Ghulam Ali, 1973), pp. 11–12.

6 Tara Chand, *History of the Freedom Movement in India,* Vol. III, (New Delhi: Publications Division, Ministry of Information and Broadcasting 1972), pp. 252–53.

Meanwhile, the Simon Commission Report, released in May 1930, recommended the establishment of representative government in the Provinces and suggested maintaining separate Communal electorates until Hindu-Muslim tensions subsided. However, due to widespread opposition to the Simon Commission and escalating communal tensions, the British Government sought to incorporate Indian public opinion into its approach to Constitutional Reforms.

This set the stage for the three Round Table Conferences (RTCs) held in London between 1930 and 1932. While the Indian National Congress declined to participate in the First (and the Third) RTC, Dr Ambedkar, along with Rao Bahadur Srinivasan, appeared on behalf of the Depressed Classes of India and attended all three RTCs.

The RTCs primarily focused on two key questions regarding the proposed Constitutional Reform:

(i) Should India have a responsible government, and if so, when and to whom should that government be responsible?

(ii) What form should the proposed representative government take?

First Round Table Conference

The first Round Table Conference was held in London between November 1930 and January 1931. It was inaugurated by King George V on 12 November 1930 and chaired by the then Prime Minister MacDonald.

This was the first instance of a meeting arranged between the British and the Indians as equals. Gandhiji was still in jail when the announcement for the RTC was made. Although the Indian National Congress declined to attend, many other Indian groups were represented, including delegates from Princely States, the All India Muslim League, The Hindu Mahasabha, Sikhs, Parsis, Depressed

Classes and others. A total of 89 delegates from India attended the First RTC, including 57 political leaders from British India and 16 delegates from the Princely States. The three British political parties were represented by 16 delegates.

The First RTC started with six plenary meetings where delegates put forth their issues. Nine sub-committees were formed to address various matters, including Federal Structure, Provincial Constitution, Defence Services and Minorities. The idea of an All-India Federation was brought to the forefront of discussions by Tej Bahadur Sapru,[7] and all attending groups supported this concept.

Dr Ambedkar played an extensive role in both the plenary sessions and four sub-committees—Provincial Constitution, Franchise, Minorities and Defence.

Opening Plenary Session

In the opening plenary session of the First RTC, Dr Ambedkar articulated a case for political power for the Depressed Classes. At the outset, Dr Ambedkar put forth his perspective on the set of circumstances of the Depressed Classes in India. He said:[8] "The Depressed Classes form a group by themselves, which is distinct and separate from the Mohammedans, and, although they are included among the Hindus, they in no sense form an integral part of that community … ."

Dr Ambedkar explained that Untouchability of the Depressed Classes involves "… a positive denial of all equality of opportunity" and "most elementary … civic rights on which all human existence depends". According to him, "such a community, as large as the

7 V.P. Menon, *The Transfer of Power in India* (Delhi: Orient Longman, 1957), p. 44.

8 For full text of the Speech, see Jadhav, *Ambedkar Speaks,* Vol. III, pp. 101-07

population of England or of France, and so heavily handicapped in the struggle for existence, cannot but have some bearing on the right sort of solution of the political problem."

Dr Ambedkar concluded with an impassioned demand for a democratic Republic for India. He said:

> … We must have a government in which people in power will give their undivided allegiance to the best interests of the country, … which … will not be afraid to amend the social and economic code of life which the dictates of justice and expediency so urgently call for. This role the British Government will never be able to play. It is only a government which is of the people, for the people and by the people that will make this possible …

Dr Ambedkar further pressed for the need for a *Swaraj* Constitution, asserting, "… We feel that nobody can remove our grievances as well as we can, and we cannot remove them unless we get political power in our own hands … It is only in a *Swaraj* Constitution that we stand any chance of getting the political power into our own hands, without which we cannot bring salvation to our people."

Dr Ambedkar then brought up a number of apprehensions regarding the uncertain future of the Depressed Classes. While expressing support for Dominion Status for India, he sought clarifications on crucial matters: "How will Dominion India operate? Where will the centre of political power be? Who will have it? Will the Depressed Classes have a rightful claim to it?"

Emphasizing that these questions are a matter of "chief concerns", he argued that "… the Indian Society is a gradation of Castes forming an ascending scale of reverence and a descending scale of contempt." This system, he demonstrated, "gives no scope for the growth of that sentiment of equality and fraternity so essential for a democratic form of government".

Dr Ambedkar even drew outlines for the future Constitution. He stressed that "... the political mechanism ... must have a definite relation to the psychology of the society for which it is devised". Otherwise, the Constitution drawn up could be "a total misfit to the society for which it is designed ...".

Dr Ambedkar supported *Swaraj* but with a critical rider. He indicated that no thought has been given to the claim of the Depressed Classes for political power and added: "Although we want responsible government, we do not want a government that will only mean a change of masters. Let the Legislature be fully and really representative if your Executive is going to be fully responsible."

At the conclusion of his speech, Dr Ambedkar declared: "... Depressed by the Government, suppressed by the Hindu and disregarded by Muslims, we [the Depressed Classes] are left in a most intolerable position of utter helplessness to which I am sure there is no parallel ... ."

Dr Ambedkar's speech was applauded. His clarity, articulation and fearlessness invited admirers. The *Indian Daily Mail* commended the speech as one of the finest bits of oratory during the whole Conference.[9]

* * *

On Franchise and Suffrage

During the meeting of the sub-committee on Franchise (22 December 1930), Dr Ambedkar made a compelling case for adult franchise and also expounded on the controversial question of joint electorates *versus* separate electorates. Dr Ambedkar resolutely

9 Keer, *Dr Ambedkar* (2005).

expressed his perspective that the then proposed Dominion Status must be accountable to the people of India as a whole. He said:[10] "... Speaking on behalf of the Depressed Classes, I cannot honestly consent to responsible government or to Dominion Status unless I can be sure that the people for whom I speak are to have a place in that Constitution ... ."

On the issue of adult suffrage, Dr Ambedkar called it "the inherent right of every individual". According to him,

> When you give an individual the franchise, ... you give him the power to regulate the terms on which he will live in a relationship with other individuals in society. ... surely you cannot give it to only the higher Classes, or the propertied Classes ... and leave the lower Classes at their mercy. ... it cannot be a one-sided bargain; ...

Dr Ambedkar's spirit of Classical Republicanism becomes very visible here. He emphatically maintained that in India there can't be "any system of suffrage short of adult suffrage which will give equality of representation to all the Castes and communities in India;...". He warned: "....surely you do not want to create a system of political government in which only some Castes and some communities will predominate... ."

On Joint *versus* Separate Electorates

Regarding the "thorny" issue of Joint *versus* Separate Electorates,[11] Dr Ambedkar opined that the "question of Joint *versus* Separate

---

10 Proceedings of Sub-Committee No. VI (Franchise), Govt of India, Central Publication Branch, Calcutta, 1931, pp.28-35.

11 Separate Electorates: the voting population of a country or region is divided into different electorates, based on certain factors such as religion, caste, gender and occupation. Here, members of each

electorates is inseparable from the question of franchise". He cautioned that it will not be possible to "ask, compel and get the consent of any minority in India to agree to joint electorates unless that minority has adult suffrage".

He vehemently clarified, "I am not going to place myself under the thumb and authority of any majority government, unless I am certain that I can exercise electoral power in elections which is commensurate with my social power. ..."

On the Issue of Minority Representation

Dr Ambedkar and his peer Rao Bahadur Srinivasan deemed it wise to submit a detailed Memorandum outlining the specific political safeguards desired by the Depressed Classes in the future Constitution of India. This Memorandum, titled 'A Scheme of Political Safeguards for the Protection of the Depressed Classes in the Future Constitution of a Self-governing India', was disseminated among the Members of the Sub-Committee on Minorities.[12]

The Memorandum aimed to secure for the Depressed classes not only the basic rights of citizenship shared by other citizens but also a "Fundamental Right" engrained in the Constitution, focused on the abolition of Untouchability and the establishment of equality of citizenship, along with a mechanism for redressal. Further, it outlined

---

electorate vote only to elect representatives for their electorate. Separate electorates are different from Reserved System of seats, where certain numbers of seats in a Legislature are reserved for a minority group.

12 For the full text of the Memorandum, see Jadhav (ed), *Ambedkar Writes*, Vol. I, pp. 84-92. For the full text of the relevant speech, see Jadhav (ed), *Ambedkar Speaks,* Vol. III, pp. 122-28. Proceedings of the Sub-Committee No. III (Minorities), Govt of India, Central Publication Branch, Calcutta, 1931, pp.73-80; BAWS, Vol. 2, pp. 528-56.

conditions regarding electoral law, advocating for the Right to adequate representation in both Provincial and Central Legislatures, the Right to elect their own people as their representatives through (1) adult suffrage and (2) initially through separate electorates for the first 10 years followed by joint electorates with reserved seats.

Closing Plenary Session

Dr Ambedkar's observations during the closing plenary session were notably sharp, analytically compelling and yet passionately delivered.[13] He vehemently criticized the Committee's report for its failure to grant franchise to all adults, reiterating his stance that a responsible government must be truly representative. He expressed shock at the reluctance, stating, "it was difficult to persuade even the Indian Liberals to consent to enfranchise 25 per cent of the population for Provincial Legislatures." Expressing his alarm about the same in respect of the Central Legislature, Dr Ambedkar cautioned: "A franchise so limited must necessarily make the future Government of India, a government of the masses by the Classes."

Dr Ambedkar chastised the British Rule for the "impasse" regarding the distribution of seats between the majority and various minority communities, attributing it to the "mischief done in the past ... The British government set different values on different communities according to the political use they made of them and gave to many communities an extraordinary share of political power by denying it to the Depressed Classes ...".

Ambedkar further stated, "the most aggrieved community is the Depressed Classes, ... I was hoping that this Conference would

13 For the full text of the relevant speech, see Jadhav (ed), *Ambedkar Speaks,* Vol. III, pp. 131-34. 'Proceedings of the RTC (1930-31), The Plenary Session (General Review)', 19 January 1931, pp. 438-41; BAWS, Vol. 2, pp. 596-99.

proceed on the principle that what is wrongly settled is never settled, and give to the Depressed Classes their rightful quota of seats ... But this has not happened... ."

Dr Ambedkar deplored that the claims of the Depressed Classes "have just been heard, not even been adjudged and I do not know how many of them will be admitted". He raised alarm that "the claims of the Depressed Classes for representations may be whittled down to satisfy the ever-increasing scramble by other communities who are manoeuvring not so much for protection as for power".

In a passionate conclusion, Dr Ambedkar said: "Our aim is to realize in practice our ideal of one man, one value in all walks of life—political, economic and social. It is because a representative government is one means to that end that the Depressed Classes attach to it a great value... ."

He added, "You may tell me that the Depressed Classes have your sympathy. For a stricken people what is wanted is something more concrete, something more defined. You may despise me for being unduly apprehensive. My reply is it is better to be despised for too anxious apprehensions than to be ruined by too confident a security."

* * *

During the First RTC, Dr Ambedkar emerged as a fervent nationalist, advocating that Independence from British Rule was essential for fostering an egalitarian, Caste-free society. His vision went beyond mere transfer of power to Indians; he aimed to building a democratic nation, aligning with the ideals of Mahatma Phule, Periyar and other leaders of the anti-Caste movement. Dr Ambedkar dreamt of an Indian society that was democratic and Republican, built upon the principles of liberty, equality and fraternity.[14]

---

14 Gail Omvedt makes a similar observation in p. 39 of his book, *Ambedkar: Towards an Enlightened India* (Delhi: Penguin, 2004).

Beyond the formal proceedings of the RTC, Dr Ambedkar actively engaged with the foreign press, giving interviews and contributing articles to foreign journals. He also addressed several small gatherings, including those of the British Parliament Members. Dr Ambedkar seized the opportunity to draw attention to the deplorable conditions faced by the Depressed Classes in India, effectively bringing their plight to the attention of thought leaders in the Western world. The world opinion became quite supportive. *Sunday Chronicle,* for example, paid a glowing tribute to Dr Ambedkar for his contribution to the RTC.

Dr Ambedkar's role in the First RTC and his brilliant presentations at the Conference gave him wide publicity in Europe and in America.

* * *

In terms of tangible outcomes from the First RTC, it was difficult to make progress at the Conference given the absence of the representatives of the Congress. Further, little was done to implement the recommendations from the Conference in view of the continued Civil Disobedience in India. The British Government recognized that the participation of the Indian National Congress was crucial for any fruitful discussion on the future of Constitutional Government in India. In fact, Prime Minister MacDonald during the closing session of the First Round Table Conference went on to express the hope that the Congress Party would be represented at the next session of the Round Table Conference.

Gandhi-Irwin Pact and Karachi Resolution

Taking a cue from the British Prime Minister, Viceroy Irwin promptly ordered the unconditional release of Gandhiji and other members of the Congress Working Committee. The Viceroy then invited the Congress for a discussion, and the Congress Working Committee nominated Gandhiji to hold the negotiations on their behalf. The result of these discussions is known as the Gandhi-Irwin Pact, which was signed on 14 February 1931.

The Viceroy agreed to all but two demands of the Congress. The rejected demands were 1) public inquiry into police excesses and 2) substitution of Bhagat Singh and his comrades' death sentence to life sentence.[15] In turn, the Congress agreed to dissolve the Civil Disobedience Movement and participate in the next RTC.

In March 1931, a Special Session of the Congress convened in Karachi to endorse the Gandhi-Irwin Pact. This gathering happened shortly after the execution of Bhagat Singh, Sukhdev and Rajguru. The Karachi Session primarily aimed to honour the courage of the martyrs, affirm the Gandhi-Irwin Pact, reaffirm *Purna Swaraj* as the ultimate objective, and approve the Karachi Resolution document.[16]

The Karachi Resolution document reiterated the Congress Party's commitment to *Purna Swaraj* or 'complete Independence'. In addition to Fundamental Rights, the Resolution included a list of socio-economic principles/rights whose adherence shall be the duty of the State. Some of these provisions included abolishing of child labour, protection of women workers, free Primary Education, etc. It is pertinent to note that these provisions in the Karachi Resolution went on to exert some influence on the Constituent Assembly later while formulating the Directive Principles of State Policy.

Second Round Table Conference

Between the First and the Second Sessions of the Round Table Conference, there was a change in the political landscape both in

---

15 A nagging question, undoubtedly with the benefit of hindsight, could Gandhiji not have insisted on reducing the punishment for Bhagat Singh and others to life sentence instead of death sentence.

16 https://inc.in/en/inc-timeline/1925-1935

Britain and India. In England, the Labour Government was replaced by an uneasy coalition between the Labour and Conservatives. Despite this change, MacDonald remained the Prime Minister of Britain. In India, Lord Willingdon took over from Lord Irwin as the Viceroy, and Samuel Hoare was appointed as the Secretary of State for India. During this period, the Labour leadership was still sympathetic towards the Indian demand for Dominion Status. However, the Conservatives, led by Winston Churchill, strongly opposed negotiations between the British Government and the Congress. Instead, they advocated for a strong government in India.

Against this political backdrop, the Second Round Table Conference took place in London from 7 September 1931 to 1 December 1931. The Indian National Congress nominated Mahatma Gandhi as its sole representative. He was accompanied by Madan Mohan Malviya and Sarojini Naidu.

When the Second Session of the Round Table Conference began on 7 September 1931, nobody anticipated the vitriolic debate that unfolded between Gandhiji and Dr Ambedkar. But it did. The contentious issue at hand was whether to grant separate electorates for the Depressed Classes.

The Session faced a deadlock on the issue of minority representation. The failure to reach consensus among the various delegate groups meant that the conference yielded no substantial results for India's Constitutional future. Instead, the British Government, rejecting India's demand for freedom, introduced, among other measures, a unilateral British Communal Award, paving the way for the creation of two Muslim-majority Provinces.

After the failure of the Second Session of the Round Table Conference, the Congress Working Committee took a major decision on 29 December 1931 to restart the Civil Disobedience Movement.

Subsequently, on 4 January 1932, Gandhiji was arrested and was put in Yerawada Jail, Pune.

Gandhiji was still in jail when British Prime Minister MacDonald announced the long-awaited Communal Award on 16 August 1932, which granted Separate Electorates for Untouchables and allocated them 78 seats in the Provincial Council.

It was here that Gandhiji initiated a "fast unto death" in protest against the Communal Award. It was during this protest that the historic Poona Pact was signed between Gandhiji and Dr Ambedkar.

Gandhiji ultimately decided to withdraw the Civil Disobedience Movement in April 1934.

Third Round Table Conference

The Third Session of the Round Table Conference, held in London from 17 November 1932 to 24 December 1932, was not attended by the Indian National Congress and Gandhiji. Many other Indian leaders also chose to disregard it. Similar to the preceding sessions, this Conference yielded little tangible outcome from its deliberations.

The recommendations of the Round Table Conferences were compiled into a White Paper in March 1933 and subsequently debated in the British Parliament. Subsequently, a Joint Select Committee was formed to scrutinize the proposed recommendations and draft a new Act for India. This Committee presented a draft Bill in February 1935, which came into effect in July 1935, as the Government of India Act, 1935.

Lothian Committee on Indian Franchise

Following the recommendations by the Franchise Sub-Committee of the Round Table Conference, the Indian Franchise Committee was constituted in December 1931. Lord Lothian, the British Parliamentary Under Secretary of State for India, chaired the Committee, which comprised 18 members, including Dr Ambedkar.

Dr Ambedkar's submission to the Lothian Committee (1 May 1932), published in the Report of the Indian Franchise Committee, may be summarised as follows:[17]

1. The term 'Depressed Classes' is 'vague'. It includes others who are not strictly Untouchables. It should be confined to Untouchables only.
2. The term 'Depressed Classes' is 'inappropriate and unsuitable'. Until better expression is found, the Untouchables should be described by the more expressive term 'Exterior Castes' or 'Excluded Castes' and not as Depressed Classes.
3. In order to ascertain the Untouchables, it would be quite inappropriate to apply the same test(s) uniformly all over India. Untouchability is 'a matter of social behaviour and which must therefore vary with the circumstances of each Province'. Ignoring this fact and applying the test(s) of Untouchability in absolute uniformity 'is simply to trifle with the problem.'
4. Insisting upon the application of uniform test(s) of Untouchability all over India is not only inappropriate but also futile. 'If our aim is to demarcate the class of people who suffer from social odium, then it matters very little which test we apply.' This is because 'each of these tests is indicative of

17 'Franchise and Tests of Untouchability' (Submission by Dr Ambedkar to the Indian Franchise Committee) From 'Indian Franchise (Lothian) Committee' 1931-32: Vol. 1 Report and appendices. London, Calcutta, 1932. Accessed from https://discovery.nationalarchives.gov.uk/

the same social attitude on the part of the Touchables towards the Untouchables'.

5. There is a clear difference between Untouchability in its 'literal and notional sense'. 'Untouchability in its notional sense persists even where Untouchability in its literal sense has ceased to obtain'. The test of Untouchability must, therefore, be applied in its notional sense.

CHAPTER ELEVEN

The Government of India Act, 1935 and Proposed Federation of India

In 1932, when the Communal Award was announced, a faction of Congress leaders vehemently opposed its provisions for minorities. Among them, notable figures like Madan Mohan Malaviya and Madhav Shrihari Aney decided to break away from the Congress and floated a new party called the Congress Nationalist Party in 1934.[1]

It was around this time that the 1934 general elections were held in British India. This election also introduced female suffrage, granting women the right to vote. The Indian National Congress emerged as the largest party, closely followed by the Congress Nationalist Party. However, the election also witnessed a significant number of independent candidates, particularly from Muslim constituencies, getting elected. The leadership of the Muslim independents was assumed by Jinnah, who revived the nearly defunct Muslim League after the election. Before this, Jinnah had retreated from active politics. He had attended the first two sessions

---

1 'Major Elections, 1920-1945' in A Historical Atlas of South Asia, Joseph E. Schwartzberg (ed). https://dsal.uchicago.edu/reference/schwartzberg/fullscreen.html?object=110. (accessed 24 May 2020).

of the Round Table Conference and remained stationed in London from 1930 to 1934, where he had set up his legal practice. However, in early 1934, he decided to move back to the subcontinent and resume his role in politics.

In April 1934, Gandhiji and the Congress withdrew the Civil Disobedience Movement. Following this, Gandhiji announced his retirement from active politics, and tendered his resignation from the Congress Party. Gandhiji believed that stepping down from Congress was necessary to better serve its principles in thought, word, and action. He wanted to dedicate himself fully to working within the rural communities.

Under the circumstances, the Congress was broadly deliberating on resorting to various avenues in the short term. Some leaders advocated that constructive work on Gandhian lines should continue. Another section wanted to continue with constitutional struggle through the work in the Councils. Then there was yet another section of Leftist leaders in the Congress who were keen to continue the mass struggle and put continuous pressure on the British Government.

Amidst this internal tussle in the Congress, the Government of India Act was passed by the British Parliament in August 1935. The Act had some 11 'Parts' and 10 'Schedules'. A few significant features of the Act are included:

1. A significant measure of autonomy was granted to the Provinces of British India. Under the Government of India Act, 1935, Provincial Autonomy was going to be inaugurated through election. This ended the system of dyarchy at the Provincial level, introduced by the Government of India Act, 1919.
2. Dyarchy was introduced at the Central level; key subjects like defence and foreign affairs were under the direct control of the Governor General.

3. The Act contained a provision for the formation of a 'Federation of India'. The Federation was proposed to consist of two levels: a Central Executive and Parliament, and below it, Provinces and Princely States.
4. Provision of separate electorates for Muslims, Sikhs and others.
5. The Depressed Classes were granted the quota of reserve seats as per the Poona Pact.
6. The franchise was widened from 3 per cent to around 14 per cent of the population.
7. Critical emergency powers rested with the Governor.[2]

Lord Linlithgow was appointed as the new Viceroy with the responsibility of bringing the Act into effect. As per the Act, Provincial Elections were held in 1937 and thus began an era of Provincial Autonomy in India.

* * *

The 1935 Act was condemned by a majority of sections and unanimously rejected by the Congress. The Congress demanded convening of a Constituent Assembly elected on the basis of adult franchise to frame a Constitution for Independent India. The Muslim League also expressed reservations against the Act but was ready to work with the Provincial sections for "what it was worth".[3] However,

---

2 Centre for Law and Policy Research 2017, 'Government of India Act 1935'. Constituent Assembly Debates. https://www.constitutionofindia.net/historical_constitutions/government_of_india_act_1935_2nd%20August%201935. (accessed 24 May 2020).

3 *Ibid.*

some organizations like the Hindu Mahasabha and the National Liberal Foundations were in favour of the provisions of the Act.[4]

In its sessions at Lucknow in early 1936 and then Faizpur later that year, the Congress decided to fight the upcoming elections. The decision on office acceptance was postponed to the post-election phase. Gandhiji rejoined the Congress in the Lucknow Session under the Presidency of Jawaharlal Nehru.[5]

Provincial Elections, 1937

As stipulated in the Government of India Act, 1935, Provincial elections took place in British India during the winter of 1936-37. These elections were the first instance where a larger number of Indians than ever before were eligible to participate. The results were declared in February 1937, with the Indian National Congress emerging victorious in all Provinces except Bengal, Assam, Punjab, Sindh, and the NWFP. Nonetheless, it still remained the single largest party in Bengal, Assam, and the NWFP. The All-India Muslim League failed to form a government in any Province.

The Congress Ministries, established after the elections in 1937, held office until October and November 1939, when they resigned in objection to India being dragged into World War II without consulting its people and to protest against Viceroy Lord Linlithgow's unilateral declaration of India as belligerent.

Dr Ambedkar's Entry into Electoral Politics

In the meantime, Dr Ambedkar revamped his strategy to integrate the Depressed Classes in the new institutional framework outlined

---

4 *Ibid.*

5 Bipan Chandra, *India's Struggle for Independence 1857–1947* (New Delhi; New York: Penguin Books, 1989).

by the Government of India Act, 1935. He took a significant step by founding his first political party, the Independent Labour Party (ILP), with the intention of participating in the proposed, first-ever Provincial elections announced in August 1936.

When asked what prompted him to select that particular name for the party, Dr Ambedkar clarified that the party would operate independently of any other political organization, yet it would be open to collaboration with any party where feasible. He described the party as a labour organization, emphasizing its primary goal to enhance the welfare of the Labouring Classes.

In the first-ever general elections to the Bombay Legislative Assembly, held in February 1937, ILP fielded 18 candidates in the Bombay Province—12 on reserved seats and six on general seats. In addition, 14 candidates ran for election in the Central Provinces. Despite being a new party, the performance was above par—15 candidates secured victory in the Bombay Province, with 12 of them hailing from the Depressed Classes. Interestingly, the Congress nominee, who contested against Dr Ambedkar, was a famous cricket player, P. Balu (formerly Palvankar, a name he had changed to conceal his Untouchable background). Dr Ambedkar emerged victorious with unequivocal majority, thus marking the commencement of his stint as an elected Legislator in Bombay Legislative Assembly.

* * *

Proposed Federation of India

As mentioned earlier, the Government of India Act, 1935, had a very important provision, i.e., the establishment of a 'Federation of India' composed of both British India and the Indian 'Princely States'.

After the first-ever Provincial elections held in 1936-37, Viceroy Linlithgow set out to garner support for the proposed 'Federation of India' as per the Government of India Act, 1935.

There was a lot of debate in the country regarding the so-called 'Scheme of All-India Federation' among all political parties. All political parties, it seems, were aware of the "defects" in the Scheme. Nevertheless the Congress was not opposed to the idea, apparently, because it was hoped that with certain changes made in the Constitution of the Federation beforehand, it could be made workable.[6]

While the debate regarding acceptability of the proposed 'Federation of India' was going on, Dr Ambedkar delivered a public address[7] wherein he explained the "Scheme" and examined it critically in the light of "accepted tests of democratic federations in operation elsewhere in the world".

Dr Ambedkar's incisive analysis of the 'Scheme of Federation of India' may be summarized as under:

1. Monstrous Size

According to Dr Ambedkar, the proposed Federation of India was going to be "really a monster among federations". Of the five countries who had adopted the federal form of government then, i.e., the United States of America, Switzerland, Germany, Canada and Australia, "in terms of area, the Indian Federation would be $3/5^{th}$ of the US and Australia, half of Canada, 9 times of Germany and 120 times of Switzerland"; whereas in terms of population, it would be "3 times of the US, 5 times of Germany, 35 times of Canada, 58 times of Australia and 88 times of Switzerland".

6 It may be recalled that the idea was proposed in the RTC by Tej Bahadur Sapru, a prominent Congress leader.

7 Kale Memorial Lecture at the Gokhale Institute of Politics and Economics in Pune (29 January, 1939). The address was also published as a book in the same year, titled *Federation Versus Freedom*. Available at BAWS, Vol. 1, Summary available in Jadhav: *Ambedkar Speaks*, Vol. I, 2014, pp 100-113.

2. Federation and the Unity of India

Dr Ambedkar admitted that the "advantages of a common system of government are indeed very real. To have a common system of law, administration and a feeling of oneness are some of the essentials of good life".

Raising a question on "how much of this Indian India is going to be brought under this Federation?", Dr Ambedkar pointed out that many would be inclined to believe that "every inch of this area will be included in the Federation and will be subject to the authority of the Federal Government". Not really. He explained that the total number of the Princely States which can join the Federation would be 147. "This means 480 States will remain outside the Federation and can never become a part of Federation, as the total number of States is 627. This shows that the Federation is not an All-India Federation," he said.

Under the Scheme, the people in the Indian Princely States would remain the subjects of the States. The Federal Government cannot deal with them directly. Everything has to be done through the Ruler of the Princely State. Dr Ambedkar asked: "How can a feeling that they belong to the national Government grow in the subject of the Indian [Princely] States if they are excluded from any and every influence, and are not even made to feel the existence of the National Government." He, therefore, argued that "United States of India will not be more than a mere body of United States. It has no potentiality of forging a nation out of these [Princely] States".

3. Democratization of Autocracies

Dr Ambedkar pointed out that "one of the advantages of the Federal Scheme which is claimed by its protagonists is that it brings beneath the dome of a single political edifice the new democracies of British India and the ancient autocracies of the Indian States, and that by bringing the two under one edifice, it provides contact between democracy and autocracy, and thus enables the democracy in British India to democratize the autocracies in the Indian States".

According to Dr Ambedkar, the outcome would be to the exact opposite. "[The Princely] States are placed by law in a position to control affairs of British India and by the same law British India is disabled from exercising any influence over the States. So this will not result in democratization of the Indian States. On the other hand, it helps the Indian States to destroy democracy in British India."

4. Federation and Responsibility

According to Dr Ambedkar, the Federal Scheme is a case of limited responsibility. The reason being, "the Lower and the Upper Chamber have members nominated by the Rulers of the [Princely] States, and these seats may be filled on the advice of the political department of the Government, which exercises its power on behalf of the Crown. These representatives will be under the control of the Viceroy, so the Legislature is not independent in all senses".

5. The Bane of the Federal Scheme

According to Dr Ambedkar, "a real Federation must ... consist of free units enjoying more or less the same measure of freedom and civil liberty, and representation by the democratic process of election". He advocated that the participation of the Indian [Princely] States in the Federation should be similar to that of the Provinces "in the establishment of representative institutions and responsible Government, civil liberties and method of election to the Federal Houses". Or else, he warned that "the Federation as it is now contemplated, will, instead of building up Indian unity, encourage separatist tendencies and involve the States in internal and external conflicts ...".

According to Dr Ambedkar, the fundamental question really was whether the Federal Scheme "is capable of so evolving, that in the end, India will reach her goal. Imperfections there are bound to be. But … a distinction must be drawn between imperfections and inherent and congenital deficiencies. Imperfections can be removed … ", while the deficiencies cannot.

Dr Ambedkar argued that the "greatest deficiency in the Constitution [of the Federation] is that it will not lead to Dominion Status … . If the Princes object to the grant of Dominion Status to India, then India cannot get Dominion Status. The destiny of India will [thus] be controlled by the Princes".

Moreover, Dr Ambedkar argued, "under the Government of India Act, neither the Federal Legislature nor the Provincial Legislature has any powers of altering or amending the Constitution [of the Federation]." And even "… if the Parliament amended any of the provisions of the Act … the Princes would get the right to secede from the Federation …".

According to Dr Ambedkar: "Some people with Republican faith in them desire their total abolition ... The cure for this ill is not a popular government. It is the lack of resources which is the problem … ." Dr Ambedkar illustrated that as many as 566 out of 627 States had annual revenue less than Rs 10 lakh and therefore, were incapable of providing public welfare as well as law and order services.

The only way out according to him was "to reorganize the whole area occupied by the Indian States. The proper solution would be to fix an area of a certain size and of certain revenue and to constitute it into a new Province, and to pension off the rulers now holding any territory in that area".[8] Dr Ambedkar also warned: "The States cannot

---

8 Isn't this precisely what Vallabhbhai Patel did as the First Home Minister of Independent India and what Indira Gandhi did in 1971

be reorganized after accession because when they are admitted into the Federation that means their sovereign status is recognized. That means its right to integrity of its territory and to guaranteeing of its powers of internal administration."

* * *

The debate on the proposed Federation came to an abrupt halt in September 1939 when the then Viceroy Linlithgow proclaimed a state of war between India and the Nazi forces. On 11 September 1939, the Viceroy announced the British Government's decision to hold the proposed Federation under suspension. Subsequently, when Provincial governments of Congress resigned *en masse*, the process of Constitutional Reforms went into a limbo until the arrival of the Cripps Mission in 1942.

---

as the Prime Minister, abolishing "Privy Purses"? This is yet another example of Dr Ambedkar thinking ahead of his times, which has gone unrecognized.

CHAPTER TWELVE

Cripps Mission (1942) and Constitutional Reforms

In March 1942, amidst the escalating Japanese threat in Asia, British Prime Minister Winston Churchill appointed a new mission to negotiate a political settlement in India. Apparently, Churchill felt "compelled" to send this mission under pressure from the US and other Allied Forces, aiming to secure India's active participation in World War II.

Sir Stafford Cripps, a member of Churchill's War Cabinet, headed the Mission with the objective of reaching an agreement with Mahatma Gandhi and Jinnah to garner India's full participation and support for the British war effort, in exchange for a promise of granting full self-government after the war.

During his three-week stay in India, Sir Cripps organized meetings with leaders representing various communities including Sikhs, Muslims, Princes and Depressed Classes. He also engaged in extensive discussions with prominent Congress figures such as Gandhi, Nehru and Maulana Azad, who was the President of the Congress at the time.

Although Cripps asserted that the British policy in India aimed for "the earliest possible realization of self-government in India", the Draft Declaration he presented faced significant opposition. This Declaration pledged the formation of an Indian Union with Dominion Status and the establishment of a Constituent Assembly to draft a new Constitution. The members of this Assembly were to be elected by the Provincial Assemblies, with nomination rights extended to the Rulers in the case of Princely States. Addressing the demand for Pakistan, the Declaration allowed provinces unwilling to accept the proposed Constitution to negotiate separate agreements with Britain regarding their future status.

As expected, negotiations between the Cripps Mission and Congress leaders ended in complete failure. The Congress vehemently objected to the proposal for Dominion Status instead of full Independence and opposed the representation of Princely States in the proposed Constituent Assembly by the nominees of their Rulers rather than by the people of the States. Most significantly, they strongly opposed the provision for the Partition of India.

At the end, the British Government spurned the demand for the immediate transfer of effective power to the Indians. The primary reason for the failure of the negotiations lay in the Cripps Mission's inability to engage in meaningful bargaining and negotiation. Apparently, the Mission had been instructed not to deviate from the Draft Declaration. The adoption of a rigid "take it or leave it" stance made operationally meaningful negotiations practically impossible.

Cripps had to return to England, leaving the Congress leaders feeling both angry and frustrated. Despite their ongoing sympathy for the victims of Fascist aggression, there was a growing sentiment that the time had come for a final assault on Imperialism.

The breakdown of the Cripps Mission negotiations sparked widespread resentment among the Indian populace. Their agony was worsened further by wartime shortages and inflation. With Japanese forces threatening India's borders, the terrifying prospect of a conquest of India by another foreign power seemed imminent.

From April to August 1942, tensions escalated nationwide, and the Congress, under the Gandhiji's leadership, resolved to take strong action to pressurize the British Government to accept the Indian demand for full Independence.

During the All-India Congress Committee meeting in Mumbai on 8 August 1942, the now famous 'Quit India Resolution' was passed. It emphatically declared, *inter alia*: "... the immediate ending of the British rule in India is an urgent necessity ... The ending of British rule in this country is a vital and immediate issue on which depends the future of the War and the success of freedom and democracy ...".

During his speech to the Congress delegates that evening, the unusually militant Gandhiji, *inter alia,* stated:

> I am not going to be satisfied with anything short of complete freedom ... Here is a *mantra* ... You may imprint it on your hearts and let every breath of yours give expression to it. The *mantra* is: 'Do or Die'. We shall either free India or die in the attempt; we shall not live to see the perpetuation of our slavery ... .

The historic resolution also declared the decision to commence a nationwide non-violent mass struggle with Gandhi at the helm.[1] However, the British Government swiftly nipped it in the bud. In the early hours of the following day (i.e., 9 August), the Congress was declared illegal, and all prominent leaders, including Gandhi, were apprehended and detained at undisclosed locations.

This triggered a strong response from the people of India. Without leadership or formal organization to lead them, the people, especially students, peasants and workers, spontaneously coordinated *hartals*,

---

1 Both quotes above are from Chandra, *History of Modern India*, pp. 322-23.

boycotted educational institutions, conducted strikes in factories and staged demonstrations nationwide.

The British Government of India retaliated with brute force. The press was silenced, and the police and military firing reportedly resulted in approximately 10,000 casualties. India had not experienced such severe repression since the First War of Independence in 1857. After the crushing of the Revolt of 1942, there was hardly any Constitutional reform in the country till World War II ended in 1945.

* * *

The Cripps Mission and Dr Ambedkar

Like the Congress, Dr Ambedkar was also very unhappy about the proposals of the Cripps Mission, but for altogether different reasons.

Dr Ambedkar clarified his position through a press statement[2] issued in the second half of July 1942. Salient features of his press statement may be summarised as under:

1. The Mission's proposals represent a "sudden volte-face" on the part of the British Government. The proposal regarding the setting up of a Constituent Assembly proposed earlier by the Congress was, in fact, rejected by the British Government "only a few months previously".
2. The proposed Constituent Assembly "is nothing short of a betrayal of the Depressed Classes". The press statement recalled that on 23 April 1941, Mr Amery, Secretary of State for India, while referring to the Congress demand for the Constituent Assembly, had said, *inter alia*, "... the

2 For summary, see Jadhav: *Ambedkar Writes*, (2014), Vol. I, pp 189-96.

Constitution itself and the body which is to frame it must be the outcome of agreement between principal elements in India's national life".

3. In spite of such pledges given, the British Government has gone back on their "plighted" word and has conceded to the proposal for a Constituent Assembly. Just one year ago, the British Government had said that "they would not grant Constituent Assembly" because that would be a coercion of the minorities. The press statement alleged that this was being done to "win over the Congress".
4. A year ago, the British Government had said that "they will not allow Pakistan because that is Balkanization of India". Today they are prepared to allow the Partition of India.
5. According to the press statement, conceding a Constituent Assembly to the Congress and allowing the Partition of India and creation of Pakistan to the Muslim League, showed how "panic-stricken" the British Government had become in the "course of the War".
6. According to the press statement, the panic was so "great" that the British Government had conceded more than what was demanded by the Congress and Muslim League. The Congress "did not demand that the question of safeguards for the minorities should be decided by the Constituent Assembly by a mere majority vote" ... yet, the British Government had given them "the additional right to decide this minority rights issue by a bare majority vote ...". Likewise all what the Muslim League had asked was that "at the next revision of the Constitution, the *Musalmans* should not be prevented from raising the question of Pakistan", whereas the British Government have "gone a step beyond and distinctly given to the Muslim League, the right to create Pakistan".

7. On the other hand, as far as the Depressed Classes are concerned, "they are bound hand and foot, and handed over to the Caste Hindus". The Mission's proposals "offer them nothing, stone instead of bread".
8. According to the press statement, given that there are no communal quotas fixed, in the Constituent Assembly, there may not be any representatives of the Depressed Classes at all. And, even if they are there, their "voices" cannot count: they will be in a "hopeless minority" and a simple "majority vote is enough to decide any question no matter what its Constitutional importance is". In other words, the Cripps Mission's proposals "have literally thrown the Depressed Classes to the wolves".
9. The Mission's set of proposals does include the "provisions for a Treaty with the Constituent Assembly the object of which is to secure the interests of the Depressed Classes ...". According to Dr Ambedkar, a Treaty as encapsulated in the Mission's proposals "cannot override the Constitution framed by the national Government ...". Indeed, the Treaty "is going to be an empty formula, if not a cruel joke upon the Depressed Classes".

Dr Ambedkar's statement concluded with advice to the British Government: "... they should withdraw these proposals. If they cannot fight for right and justice and their plighted word, they should better make peace. They can thereby at least save their honour."

CHAPTER THIRTEEN

Sapru's *Swaraj* Constitution, Cabinet Mission and Dr Ambedkar

Continuing the tradition of *Swaraj* Constitutions from Tilak (1895) to Motilal Nehru (1928), in 1945, another proposal for a *Swaraj* Constitution emerged from the Sapru Committee Report. This report was formulated by a Committee appointed by the Non-Party Conference in November 1944, chaired by the esteemed lawyer and Congress leader Tej Bahadur Sapru.

The Sapru Committee Report[1] (1945)

The Sapru Committee was established against the backdrop of the "Communal Question", which arose from the ongoing conflict and impasse between the Congress and the Muslim League over the future of Indian Muslims. The Committee's task was "to examine the whole communal and minorities question from a Constitutional and political point of view, put itself in touch with the different parties and their leaders, including the minorities interested in the question and present a solution".

1 Based on briefs in constitutionofindia.net (accessed on 5 May 2020).

The Sapru Committee Report offered a detailed exposition on various aspects of the future Constitution of India. One section, titled 'Leading Principles of a New Constitution', resembled a constitution itself, and it included provisions relating to the Executive, Legislature, Judiciary, Public Services, etc.

Rejecting the Muslim League's call for Pakistan, the Report called for the setting up of a Constitution-making body with equal representation for Hindus and Muslims. It dismissed separate electorates for Muslims in the Union Legislature, proposing instead joint electorates with reserved seats (for Muslims). The Committee also put forth a proposal to create a 'Minorities Commission' to safeguard minority welfare and recommend corrective measures to the Government.

Interestingly, the Sapru Committee introduced a range of Fundamental Rights, including Freedom of Speech, Freedom of Press, Religious Freedom and Equality. While the content of Fundamental Rights didn't significantly differ from earlier *Swaraj* Constitutions, the Committee came up, for the first time in the Indian Constitutional history, with an idea of categorizing rights into justiciable and non-justiciable, which would play an important role in the drafting of the final Constitution of India.

Despite its merit, the Sapru Committee Report, however, received "scant attention" and failed to influence key political players. While the Muslim League was openly hostile to the report, the Congress showed lukewarm interest. Perhaps under different circumstances, the report could have garnered more attention and support.

Second Provincial Elections 1945-46

In June 1945, Viceroy Lord Wavell, who had succeeded Lord Linlithgow as Governor-General, announced the Wavell Plan, according to which some prominent leaders like Nehru, Patel and others were finally released from jails. A Conference was also convened at Simla in the last week of June 1945, to work out an interim political agreement.

In the Simla Conference, the Caste Hindus were represented by the then Congress President Maulana Abul Kalam Azad, while the Muslims were represented by Jinnah. Since he was a Member of the Viceroy's Executive Council, Dr Ambedkar could not represent the Scheduled Castes, so N. Shivraj was sent instead. Through his colleague N. Shivraj, Dr Ambedkar demanded three seats in the Central Executive of the Interim Ministry proposed to be formed. This was deemed to be justified on the basis of population and in view of the fact that Muslims were going to get five seats. The Conference could not arrive at any decision, apparently because the Congress insisted on Muslim nominees of its own.[2]

In the meantime, general elections were held in Britain in July 1945 and the Labour Party dislodged the Tories and came to power with Clement Attlee as the Prime Minister. In August 1945, Lord Wavell went to London and on his return to India in mid-September 1945, announced general elections.

* * *

The elections of 1945-46 were meant to serve two purposes:

(a) The renewal of the Provincial Assemblies, marking the first such elections since those held in 1937, and

(b) The establishment of a Constituent Assembly for the country.

This election would mark the debut of Dr Ambedkar's new political party, the Scheduled Caste Federation (SCF), as it contests the elections on a national scale, representing the Depressed Classes.

---

2 Keer, Dhananjay, *op cit*, p. 372.

Campaigning for the elections began gaining ground in October 1945. The Congress Party launched its campaign with the slogan 'Quit India', while the Muslim League's election slogan was 'Pakistan or Perish'. Both the Congress Party and the Muslim League were well-funded and had strong cadre support. In contrast, the SCF lacked both.

Dr Ambedkar travelled all over the country and made forceful speeches with passionate appeals. His election speeches in today's Maharashtra (Mumbai, Pune, Nashik, Manmad, Ahmednagar, Khandesh, Nagpur, Solapur and Satara), Gujarat (Ahmedabad) and Tamil Nadu (Chennai) received a lot of enthusiastic response.

The election results announced in March 1946, however, were most disheartening for Dr Ambedkar. They revealed a stark division along religious lines: the Congress secured victory in the general constituencies, while the Muslim League dominated nearly all Muslim seats. The SCF barely made it, winning only two seats in the Provincial Assemblies—one in Bengal and the other in the Central Province and Berar. This was a major setback for Dr Ambedkar.

* * *

Cabinet Mission

By early 1946, the British Government had apparently realized that it was no longer possible for them to keep India in bondage. On 15 March 1946, the then Prime Minister Clement Attlee, in no uncertain terms, acknowledged India's right to achieve full Independence, whether within or outside the British Commonwealth. He also said that he would not permit a minority to place their veto on the advance of the majority.

This momentous announcement prompted the dispatch of a British Cabinet Mission to India on 25 March 1946. The objective of the Mission was to devise a plan for the transfer of power from the British Government to Indian leadership. The Mission composed of three British Cabinet Ministers—Lord Pethick-Lawrence, the Secretary of State for India, Sir Stafford Cripps, and A. V. Alexander. Lord Wavell, the Viceroy of India, did not participate.

The Mission's objectives were:

(1) Holding discussions with elected representatives of British India and the Indian [Princely States] with a view to secure an agreement as to the method of framing the Constitution;
(2) Setting up a Constituent Assembly; and
(3) Establishing an Executive Council (i.e. Council of Ministers) with the support of the main Indian parties.

The Mission held meetings with the representatives of INC and Muslim League—the two major political parties in India. The dialogues tried to work out a power-sharing arrangement between Hindus and Muslims and avert a communal dispute, as well as the threat of the Partition of India. The Congress Party led by Gandhiji and Pandit Nehru demanded a strong united India with the Central Government bearing more powers as compared to the Provinces. The Muslim League led by Jinnah also wanted to keep India united, provided there were political safeguards for the Muslims such as "guarantee" of "parity" in the Legislatures.

Dr Ambedkar met the Cabinet Mission on 5 April 1946 and put forth the case for the Depressed Classes, firmly denying the allegation that they were putting a veto on India's political advancement. Dr Ambedkar, in fact, tendered a detailed memorandum to the Mission asking for the inclusion of several safeguards in the new Constitution, including separate electorates, adequate representation in the Central and Provincial Legislatures and Central and Provincial Executives, in the Public Services and on the Public Service Commissions, in addition to providing earmarked sums for the Scheduled Castes.

The Minutes of the Meeting (5 April 1946) between Dr Ambedkar and the Cabinet Mission indicate that several issues relating to the proposed Constitution were discussed, as can be seen from the following:[3]

Responding to an inquiry regarding the method of representation of the Scheduled Castes in the Constituent Assembly, Dr Ambedkar stated that "he did not want a Constituent Assembly at all". He argued that such an Assembly "would be dominated by the Caste Hindus, and the Scheduled Caste members would be no more than a small minority, which would always be outvoted even if a three-quarters or a two-thirds majority were required for the Assembly's decisions".

Dr Ambedkar suggested dividing the tasks envisioned for the Constituent Assembly into two categories: "Constitutional Questions" and "Communal Questions". As to the former, dealing with them was "beyond the mental capacity of the type of men whom Provincial Assemblies might be expected to send up, and was a job for experts". For Constitutional Questions, he proposed establishing "a commission presided over by an eminent constitutional lawyer from Great Britain or the US, supported by two Indian experts".[4]

Furthermore, Dr Ambedkar recommended that communal issues "be addressed through a conference involving leaders from different communities".

---

3 BAWS, Vol. 17 (2), pp. 189-93.

4 At that point, Dr Ambedkar, of course, did not know that the responsibility was going to be entrusted to him. His professionalism is clearly evident here.

Dr Ambedkar argued that "although the Scheduled Castes like ... the other communities had been granted separate electorates in 1932, they had virtually been deprived of them by the Poona Pact". Instead, what they had in effect was the "system of double elections which meant that in the second election, in which all the Hindus voted, the Caste Hindus could nullify the result of the first election in which Untouchables were the only voters".

Dr Ambedkar pointed out that the "Central Legislature had been in existence since 1919, yet no questions were ever asked, resolutions moved or anything else done with the object of helping the Scheduled Castes ...". He, therefore, earnestly appealed that before leaving, the British must "ensure that the new Constitution guaranteed to the Scheduled Castes the elementary human rights of life, liberty and the pursuit of happiness, and that it restored their separate electorates and gave them the other safeguards which they demanded ...".

Dr Ambedkar reiterated that as long as there were joint electorates, Scheduled Caste voters would be so few that Hindu candidates could safely ignore their wishes. Caste Hindus would never support Scheduled Caste candidates. He emphasized that "separate electorates were fundamental, since without them, the Scheduled Castes would never have their own representatives".

* * *

The Cabinet Mission proposed its plan on 16 May 1946—the 'Plan of May 16'. The Plan proposed creation of a United Dominion of India as a loose confederation of Provinces. The Cabinet Mission Plan had envisaged the election of a Constituent Assembly without giving the Scheduled Castes any guarantee of representation. Dr Ambedkar found this outrageous.

When the 'Plan of May 16' was not accepted unconditionally by both the Congress and the Muslim League, the British proposed an alternative—the 'Plan of June 16'.

The Viceroy began organizing the transfer of power to a Congress-League coalition. However, Jinnah, the leader of the Muslim League, denounced the hesitant and conditional support from the Congress and rescinded League approval for both proposed plans. Despite this setback, Congress leaders joined the newly styled Viceroy's Executive Council. The Constituent Assembly was instructed to begin its work on drafting a new Constitution for India.[5]

Dr Ambedkar's Response

Dr Ambedkar in response to the Cabinet Mission's Plan (as detailed in their statement of May 10) issued two Monographs[6] in 1946. Their salient features may be summarised, as under:

1. Ignoring the Untouchables

"The most galling and astounding feature of their proposals is their refusal to recognize the Untouchables as a separate and distinct element in the national life of India". The Mission did not even once mention the Untouchables in their statement.

2. Formation of the Constituent Assembly

Dr Ambedkar was agitated over the manner in which the members of the Constituent Assembly were going to be chosen. His statement indicated:

---

5 Elections to the Constituent Assembly of India, comprising 296 members from British Indian Provinces, were completed by August 1946—comprising 208 from the Congress and 73 from the Muslim League.

6 The two Monographs were titled: (i) A Critique of the Proposals of Cabinet Mission for Indian Constitutional Changes in so far as they affect the Scheduled Castes (Untouchables), and (ii) The Cabinet Mission and the Untouchables. For fuller summaries of these two Monographs, see Jadhav, *Ambedkar Writes*, Vol. I, pp. 406-23.

> This Constituent Assembly is to be composed of representatives chosen by the members of the Provincial Legislatures by a single transferable vote. For this purpose, the Cabinet Mission's Scheme has divided the members of the Provincial Legislatures into three categories: (1) Muslims, (2) Sikhs and (3) General—each with a fixed quota of seats. Each category has a separate electorate whereby the Muslim representatives of the Constituent Assembly will be elected by the Muslim members of the Provincial Legislature, the Sikhs by the Sikh members and the General by all the rest, including Hindus, Scheduled Castes, Indian Christians etc.

Dr Ambedkar was particularly upset because the Untouchables were not:

> Given the right to nominate their representatives in the Central Executive as has been done in the case of the Sikhs and the Muslims. In the present Interim Government, they have got two representatives of the Scheduled Castes, neither of them owe any allegiance or obligation to the Scheduled Castes. One is nominated by the Congress and the other is nominated by the Muslim League.

Dr Ambedkar also resented that the Untouchables were not "given the right to separate representation in the Constituent Assembly". "It is this discrimination, which constitutes the wrong of which the Untouchables are complaining."

3. Abrogating the Pledges

Dr Ambedkar's statement also explained how the "non-recognition of the Untouchables as a separate element by the Cabinet Mission is contrary to the pledges given to them by and on behalf of the British Government ..." and alleged that "what the Mission has done is to pamper to the prejudices of Mr Gandhi".

4. Adopting a False Criterion

The members of the Cabinet Mission had argued that "in the election, the Congress captured all seats reserved for the Untouchables; that, therefore, the Congress represented the Untouchables. That being the case, there was no justification for giving separate representation to the Untouchables".

To this, the counter-argument by Dr Ambedkar was: "The nature of the future Constitution of India was never the issue. If it had been the issue, the Congress would never have got the majority it did."

5. Way Forward

The Cabinet Mission has, by the Constitution of the Constituent Assembly, left the Untouchables entirely at the mercy of the Caste Hindus who have an absolute majority in it. The Untouchables want the restoration of separate electorates given to them by the Communal Award by His Majesty's Government and the abrogation of the Poona Pact, which was forced upon them by coercion practiced by Mr Gandhi through his fast unto death. This, the Hindus are bound to oppose.

Dr Ambedkar reasoned: "The Cabinet Mission has been advertising their proposal for an Advisory Committee on Minorities as a means of safeguarding minority rights. Anyone who examines the powers and Constitution of the Advisory Committee will know that the body is worse than useless. The device of an Advisory Committee is ... a hoax if not a humbug."

Dr Ambedkar was appalled that the Congress, in a letter addressed by it dated 15 June 1946, had taken the stand that the Untouchables were not a minority. This was an astounding proposition. For, according to Mr Gandhi's own admission in his weekly called the *Harijan* of 21 October 1939, the Untouchables were the only real minority in India. The Congress had thus taken a complete somersault, ... which was "contrary to the underlying principles of the Government of India Act, 1935, which recognizes [the Untouchables] a minority".

Concluding his statement, Dr Ambedkar earnestly appealed the British Parliament to intervene and "see that the position of the Untouchables is not jeopardised".

Dr Ambedkar proposed the following course of action:

1. Press the British Government "to make a declaration that they regard the Untouchables as a minority". Otherwise, "the Constituent Assembly dominated by the Hindus will deny them the rights of the minority", and the British Government will "be free not to come to their rescue on the ground that they were not committed to regard the Untouchables as a minority".
2. Press the British Government to declare whether they "will institute machinery, if so of what sort, to examine whether the safeguards for minorities framed by the Constituent Assembly are adequate and real ...." In this regard, the "machinery of a Joint Parliamentary Committee with power to examine witnesses from minorities communities would be most appropriate".
3. Press the British Government to announce whether they will "insist upon the Constitution framed by the Constituent Assembly containing a clause circumscribing the power of the future Indian Legislature to do away with minority safeguard by bare majority". There is no use in Parliament introducing safeguards if these safeguards can be done away with by the Indian Legislature.... "Such provisions exist in the Constitution of USA and Australia," he said.

CHAPTER FOURTEEN

Politics of Constituent Assembly and Dr Ambedkar's Own Version of Constitution

The Cabinet Mission proposed its plan on 16 May 1946 which came to be called the 'Plan of May 16'. The Plan envisaged creation of a United Dominion of India as a loose confederation of Provinces. The Cabinet Mission had also proposed a mechanism for the election of a Constituent Assembly.[1]

The British Government prepared an alternate plan—the 'Plan of June 16'—when the 'Plan of May 16' was rejected by both the Congress and the Muslim League.

The Congress had hesitantly given its approval to both plans. In view of the conditional approval by the Congress, the Muslim League revoked its approval of both plans. Nonetheless, the Congress leaders joined the restructured Viceroy's Executive Council (September 1946)—the Interim Government and Nehru became the Head (Vice-President in title, but possessing executive authority). Vallabhbhai Patel became the Member, Home (responsible for internal security

---

1 The mechanism as well as its critique by Dr Ambedkar has been discussed in Chapter 13.

and government agencies). The Congress formed governments in most Provinces, including in the NWFP and in Punjab. The League-led governments were formed in Bengal and Sindh. Instructions were given to the Constituent Assembly to begin work to write a new Constitution for India.

As expected, the Muslim League denounced the new government, and pledged to protest for the creation of a Muslim-dominated Pakistan by any means possible. Earlier, the League had organized a 'Direct Action Day' (16 August 1946), in which over 5,000 people—both Muslims and Hindus—were killed. Following the League's denouncement of the new government, again there were violent communal clashes among the Hindus, Sikhs and Muslims, in several parts of the country.

In order to contain the law and order situation and growing bloodshed, Viceroy Wavell reportedly advised Jawaharlal Nehru to convince the League to enter the government. While Patel and most Congress leaders were against the idea of aligning with the party that was under the lens for fuelling turmoil, Nehru conceded apparently in the hope of preserving communal peace.

Muslim League leaders did join the Interim Government in October 1946 with Liaquat Ali Khan at the helm, who became the Finance Minister of India. But the Interim Cabinet did not function as one team—separate meetings were held by League ministers, and both parties obstructed the major initiatives proposed by the other, engendered by their ideological differences and political hostility. The Muslim League had also decided to refuse to take part in the Constituent Assembly.

Politics of Constituent Assembly

According to the Cabinet Mission's Plan, the British Government had planned for the election of a Constituent Assembly without giving

Untouchables any guarantee of representation. When members were being elected to the Constituent Assembly by Provincial Assemblies, Dr Ambedkar hardly had a real shot with his Scheduled Caste Federation (SCF) unable to make up the required numbers. Fortunately, Jogendra Nath Mandal,[2] an SCF leader in Bengal, came forward. In a thoughtfully surprise move, he commandeered the numbers to get Dr Ambedkar elected to the Constituent Assembly from the Bengal Province (19 July 1946).

Given the apathy of the British[3] and the contempt of the Congress Party, a defeated, distressed and desperate Dr Ambedkar decided to turn his back on the British and bury the hatchet with the Congress Party. The rapprochement of Dr Ambedkar took place in the newly-elected Constituent Assembly.

Dr Ambedkar: A Turning Point in Constituent Assembly

Despite the boycott by the Muslim League, the Constituent Assembly held its first meeting on 9 December 1946 and elected Dr Rajendra Prasad as its President. On 13 December 1946, Nehru laid the foundation of the Constituent Assembly's work by moving a Resolution on the Declaration of Objectives. In a memorable speech, Nehru declared an Independent Sovereign Republic as India's objective.

During the debate on this historic Resolution, Barrister Dr M.R. Jayakar moved an amendment to postpone the vote on the Resolution

---

2 After the Partition, Mandal went to Pakistan and became temporary Chairman of Pakistan's Constituent Assembly and later Pakistan's first Minister of Law and Labour.

3 Dr Ambedkar even made a last-minute effort to connect with the British by making a trip to Britain in October 1946.

until the Muslim League members also joined the Constituent Assembly. Dr Jayakar expressed disapproval regarding the timing of the Resolution. He wanted the Muslim League to be a part of laying down the foundation of the Constitution. This amendment created a tense atmosphere in the House.

Amidst this anxious situation, Dr Ambedkar was unexpectedly invited by the Chair to speak on the issue. Dr Ambedkar seized the opportunity and rose to the occasion, literally. At the outset, he said[4] that the Resolution was akin to the age-old 'Declaration of the Rights of Man which was pronounced by the French Constituent Assembly' nearly 450 years ago.

Moving on to the issue at hand that of national unity, Dr Ambedkar while conceding that the Indian people are "divided politically, socially and economically, like a group of warring camps", said: "I am quite convinced that given time and circumstances nothing in the world will prevent this country from becoming one."

Referring to the ultimate aim of the country, Dr Ambedkar pointed out that our difficulty is "how to make the heterogeneous mass that we have today take a decision in common and march on the way which leads us to unity". In this regard, he advised the Congress Party that "it would be an act of greatest statesmanship for the majority Party even to make a concession to the prejudices of people who are not prepared to march together ...".

Dr Ambedkar even made an impassioned appeal. He said that setting slogans and strong words aside, let us bring "our opponents" in "so that they may willingly join with us on marching upon that road, which ... if we walk long enough, must necessarily lead us to unity ...".

4 Constituent Assembly Debates (CAD), Vol. 1, pp. 99-103. Also reproduced in BAWS.

Actually, what Dr Ambedkar was saying was not materially different from what Dr Jayakar had said. But Dr Ambedkar's manner of expression was statesman-like unlike Dr Jayakar's "legalistic" style.

Strongly advising one more attempt at reconciliation between the Congress and the Muslim League, Dr Ambedkar said: "When deciding the destinies of nations, dignities of people, dignities of leaders and dignities of parties ought to count for nothing. The destiny of the country ought to count for everything ... we must also consider what is going to happen with regard to the future, if we act precipitately ...".

Cautioning against acting precipitately, Dr Ambedkar stated there were only three options for solving the "Communal problem": First, surrender by one party; secondly, a negotiated peace; and thirdly "open war".

At this point, he deployed a twist. He said that he has been "hearing from certain Members of the Constituent Assembly that they are prepared to go to war" and that he was "appalled" at the idea of "solving the political problems of this country by the method of war".

Quoting Edmund Burke[5], Dr Ambedkar cautioned that if any steps were taken to resolve the Hindu-Muslim conundrum by compelling the Muslims to submit to the Constitution, possibly prepared without their consent, "this country would be involved in perpetually conquering them [ie., the Muslims]".

Dr Ambedkar again quoted Burke towards the end of his speech, "it is easy to give power, it is difficult to give wisdom."

Passionately, he added: "Let us prove by our conduct that if this Assembly has arrogated to itself sovereign powers, it is prepared to exercise them with wisdom. That is the only way by which we can

5 Edmund Burke speech, while moving his resolutions for conciliation with the British colonies (22 March 1775), Eighteenth Century Collections Online.

carry with us all sections of the country. There is no other way that can lead us to unity."

* * *

The speech elicited the longest and the most enormous applause. The speech was earnest, statesman-like and without any bitterness. The entire Assembly was enraptured by the speech and greeted it with tremendous cheer, applause and thumping of desks.

This speech was a turning point. It transformed the attitude of the Congress leaders like Jawaharlal Nehru towards Dr Ambedkar. It was music to the ears of most Congress leaders. This strategic speech changed the trajectory of Dr Ambedkar's political career.

* * *

Untouchability Abolished

On 29 April 1947, the Constituent Assembly declared: "Untouchability in any form is abolished and the imposition of any disability on that account shall be an offence." The world press commended the event as freedom for Untouchables. The *New York Times* ran the news: "The advance towards wiping out their ancient stigma has been matched in modern times only by our own abolition of slavery…." The *New York Herald Tribune* described the event as one of the fresh and clean beams of light in the post-War world.[6]

Across the globe, profuse praise was showered on Mahatma Gandhi for this great accomplishment of India. Oddly, none of the foreign journals made even a passing reference to Dr Ambedkar—who, in reality, spearheaded this great national feat.

---

6 Keer, *Dr Ambedkar: Life and Mission*, p. 393.

Dr Ambedkar's Non-official Constitution of the United States of India

While participating in the Constituent Assembly but before India's Independence on 15 August 1947, Dr Ambedkar had prepared a Memorandum titled, 'States and Minorities' and submitted it to the Constituent Assembly on behalf of his political party, the All-India Scheduled Caste Federation in March 1947.

At that time, of course, Dr Ambedkar had no idea that he would be made a Member/the Chairman of the Drafting Committee of the Indian Constitution (which actually happened on 29 August 1947). Given the timing of the submission and the format of the Memorandum, it might as well be called Dr Ambedkar's own non-official version of the proposed Indian Constitution.

* * *

Dr Ambedkar's Memorandum was couched in the form of Articles of the Constitution of the United States of India for the sake of "giving point and precision" and presented along with a lot of Explanatory Notes and Statistical material.[7]

Dr Ambedkar's non-official version of the Indian Constitution comprised a Preamble and four Articles, each with several Sections and each Section contained multiple parts and/or clauses.

The Preamble of the Constitution of the United States of India was formulated essentially on the basis of the Resolution on objectives presented by Jawaharlal Nehru (13 December 1946) and approved by the Constituent Assembly on 22 January 1947.

Article I of the proposed non-official Constitution had two Sections, with four and two clauses, respectively, dealing with a

---

7 For full details, see Jadhav, *Ambedkar Writes* (2014), pp. 424-54.

range of delicate issues related to the admission of the 600+ Indian Princely States into the United States of India.

Article II of the proposed Constitution of the United States of India had four Sections with altogether 12 clauses.

The first Section (with only one clause) identified as many as 21 Fundamental Rights of Citizens. These rights were "borrowed from the Constitutions of various countries, particularly from those wherein the conditions are more or less analogous to those existing in India".

The second Section dealt with 'Remedies against Invasion of Fundamental Rights' in four clauses:

Clause 1: Judicial Protection

Clause 2: Protection against Unequal Treatment

Clause 3: Protection against Discrimination, and

Clause 4: Protection against Economic Exploitation

As indicated in the Explanatory Notes, the Clause 1 on Judicial Protection "proposes to give protection to the citizen against Executive tyranny by investing the Judiciary with certain powers of inquisition against the abuse of authority by the Executive".

Clause 2 on 'Protection against Unequal Treatment' aims at ensuring that "all citizens shall have equal benefit of Laws, Rules and Regulations". These provisions were "borrowed from Civil Rights Protection Act, 1866 and of March 1, 1875, passed by the Congress of the United States of America to protect the Negroes against unequal treatment".

Clause 3 recognizes discrimination as a menace, "which must be guarded against if the Fundamental Rights are to be real rights. In a country like India, where it is possible for discrimination to be practiced on a vast scale and in a relentless manner, Fundamental Rights can have no meaning". Here again the remedy draws on a

Bill adopted in the US aimed at preventing "discrimination being practiced against the Negroes".

Clause 4 dealing with 'Protection against Economic Exploitation' probably formed the core of the proposed Constitution of the United States of India. As indicated in the Explanatory Notes, the "main purpose behind the Clause is to put an obligation on the State to plan the economic life of the people on lines which would lead to highest point of productivity without closing every avenue to private enterprise, and also provide for the equitable distribution of wealth".

The Clause proposes "State ownership in agriculture with a collectivized method of cultivation and a modified form of State Socialism in the field of industry. ... It also proposes to nationalize insurance ...".

As explained by Dr Ambedkar:

> The plan has two special features. One is that it proposes State Socialism in important fields of economic life. The second special feature of the plan is that it does not leave the establishment of State Socialism to the will of the Legislature. It establishes State Socialism by the Law of the Constitution and thus makes it unalterable by any act of the Legislature and the Executive....

According to Dr Ambedkar the reason for prescribing by law the shape and form of the economic structure of society ... "is to protect the liberty of the individual from invasion by other individuals, which is the object of enacting Fundamental Rights. The connection between individual liberty and the shape and form of the economic structure of society may not be apparent to everyone. Nonetheless the connection between the two is real".

Dr Ambedkar points out in the Memorandum that the challenge is to have "State Socialism without Dictatorship, to have State Socialism with Parliamentary Democracy". And the only way out is "to retain Parliamentary Democracy and to prescribe State Socialism by the Law of the Constitution so that it will be beyond the reach of a Parliamentary majority to suspend, amend or abrogate it". Thus, "one can achieve the triple object, namely, to establish socialism, retain Parliamentary Democracy and avoid Dictatorship".

The Memorandum explains the reasons for this deviation from the prevailing Constitutions which, typically, are confined "merely to prescribe the form of the political structure of society leaving the economic structure untouched. The result is that the political structure is completely set at naught by the forces, which emerge from the economic structure which is at variance with the political structure ...".

According to Dr Ambedkar:

> ... old-time Constitutional lawyers believed that the scope and function of Constitutional Law was to prescribe the shape and form of the political structure of society. They never realized that it was equally essential to prescribe the shape and form of the economic structure of society, if democracy is to live up to its principle of one man, one value.
>
> Time has come to take a bold step and define both the economic structure as well as the political structure of society by the Law of the Constitution.

The third Section (of Article II) covered 'Provisions for the Protection of Minorities' in four clauses:

Clause 1: Protection against Communal Executive.
Clause 2: Protection against Social and Official Tyranny.
Clause 3: Protection against Social Boycott.

Clause 4: Authority and obligation of the Union and State Governments to spend money for public purposes including purposes beneficial to Minorities.

Explanatory Notes clarify:

- Clause 1 has been drawn from the "American Form of Executive as a model and adapts it to Indian conditions, especially to the requirements of minorities…".
- Clause 2 provides safeguards for Minorities from "tyranny and oppression by a majority" in terms of "inquiry, publicity and discussion" on the lines as was recommended by the Sapru Committee.[8]
- Clause 3 provides protection against social boycott of minority communities, which "are taken bodily from Burma Anti-Boycott Act, 1922".
- Clause 4 provides economic protection to Minorities on the lines of Section 150 of the Government of India Act, 1935.

The fourth Section (of Article II) dealt with safeguards for the Scheduled Castes. This Section had five parts, each with multiple clauses.

Part A covered Guarantees to the Scheduled Castes with three clauses:

Clause 1: Right to Representation in the Legislature and in the Local Bodies.

Clause 2: Right to Representation in the Executive.

---

8 Sapru Committee Report has been discussed in Chapter 13.

Clause 3: Right to Representation in Services.

Explanatory Notes clarify:

- Clause 1 provides reaffirmation of the right to representation in the Legislature as in the Poona Pact. In addition, the Clause provides for reconsideration of the Quantum of Representation, Weightage and the System of Electorates.

  The clause points out that the 'quantum of representation allowed to the Scheduled Castes by the Poona Pact ... has resulted in great injustice ...".

  The clause brings out "another injustice from which the Scheduled Castes have been suffering". In this regard, there is a "double controversy. One controversy is between the majority and the minorities, the other is ... between the different minorities".

  With the existing weightage, there is unequal distribution among the various minorities. "... some minorities have secured a lion's share and some like the Untouchables have none. This wrong must be rectified by a distribution of the weightage on some intelligible principles".

  As far as the System of Electorates is concerned, the Explanatory Notes demonstrate how the Poona Pact has done a grave injustice to the Scheduled Castes and makes out a case for 'Separate Electorates' instead of the Joint Electorates. It is recommended that "If the minority decides to have separate electorates for itself, the majority cannot refuse to grant them. In other words, the majority must look to the decision of the minority and abide by it".

- Clause 2 provides for the Right to Representation in the Executive. The Clause indicates: "Experience has shown that the quantum of representation of the Scheduled Castes in the Executive should now be fixed."

- Clause 3 provides for Right to Representation in Services. It is recalled that the "demand has been admitted by the Government of India as legitimate and even the quantum of representation has been defined. All that remains is to give it a statutory basis".

Part B deals with Special Responsibilities. This part has two Clauses covering (1) Higher Education and (2) Separate Settlements for Scheduled Castes—ie., earmarking adequate financial resources.

Part C discusses 'Sanction for Safeguards and Amendment of Safeguards' with two Clauses:

Clause 1: Safeguards to be embodied in the Constitution
Clause 2: Amendment of Safeguards

Explanatory Notes clarify:

- *Clause 1* incorporates the political rights of the Scheduled Castes in the Constitution.

The Memorandum observes:

> Unfortunately for the minorities in India, Indian Nationalism has developed a new doctrine, which may be called the Divine Right of the Majority to rule the minorities according to the wishes of the majority. Any claim for the sharing of power by the minority is called communalism, while the monopolizing of the whole power by the majority is called Nationalism.... Under these circumstances, there is no way left but to have the rights of the Scheduled Castes embodied in the Constitution.

- *Clause 2* basically "replaces Clause 6 of the Poona Pact, which provides that the system of representation for the Scheduled Castes by reserved seats shall continue until determined by mutual consent between the communities concerned in the settlement. In addition, a period of 25 years has been laid down before any change could be considered".

Finally, Part D and E deal with 'Protection of SCs in Indian (Princely) States and issues relating to "interpretation", respectively.

Independence for India

On the arrival of the new Viceroy, Lord Mountbatten of Burma, in early 1947, Congress leaders reached the conclusion that a coalition between the Congress and Muslim League was unviable. This realization eventually led to the proposal and subsequent acceptance of the Partition of India.

On 3 June 1947, Lord Mountbatten announced the British Government's Plan for India's future. The Plan outlined provisions for the partition of the country; there would now be two Central Governments (i.e., Divided India and Pakistan), each with its own Constituent Assembly. Gandhiji, who had earlier considered Pakistan a sin, a patent untruth and had solemnly asked the protagonists of thr partition to "vivisect me before you vivisect India", finally relented and "instructed" Nehru (who had sought his counsel in Noakhali, East Bengal) to negotiate "an accord with Jinnah" based on "a universally acceptable and inoffensive formula for his Pakistan".[9]

---

9 Dr Ambedkar was the one who wrote the first book on the "knotty" problem of Pakistan, titled *Pakistan or Partition of India,* published first in 1940. The second edition of Dr Ambedkar's book on Pakistan, titled *Thoughts on Pakistan* became a significant reference for both sides. In the Preface to the Second Edition, Dr Ambedkar states: "The

The following week, Nehru presented a Resolution in the All India Congress Committee, which was passed by a vote of 99-52.[10]

The British Parliament enacted the Indian Independence Act on 15 July 1947 by virtue of which the Constituent Assembly became a sovereign entity. Due to the partition of Bengal, several Members, including Dr Ambedkar, lost their seats. However, with a change of heart towards Dr Ambedkar, the Congress leadership recommended him to fill the vacancy created by Barrister Jayakar's resignation[11] from the Constituent Assembly representing the Bombay Province in July 1947. Thus, Dr Ambedkar returned to the Constituent Assembly, this time with the complete backing of the Congress Party.

On 15 August 1947, India became a free nation and Dr Ambedkar was inducted into the new Cabinet of free India. Prime Minister Nehru appointed him as the Union Minister of Law, apparently under Gandhiji's insistence. Although Nehru and Patel were initially not very enthusiastic about allocating a ministerial berth to Dr Ambedkar, Gandhiji stressed the importance of his inclusion in the nation-building process.[12] This speculation was further supported by a conversation Gandhiji had with two visiting foreigners,[13] during

---

fact that Mr Gandhi and Mr Jinnah in their recent talks cited the book as an authority on the subject which might be consulted with advantage bespeaks the worth of the book ..." For summary of this book, see Jadhav (ed), *Ambedkar Writes*, Vol. I, pp.114-89.

10 Lelyveld, *op cit*, p. 310.

11 Barrister M. R. Jayakar then became the founder Vice-Chancellor of Pune University.

12 S.M. Gaikwad, 'Ambedkar and Indian Nationalism', *Economic and Political Weekly*, 7 March 1998.

13 M.S. Gore, The Social Context of an Ideology: Ambedkar's Political and Social Thought (Delhi: Sage Publications, 1993), p. 180.

which he had reportedly expressed his desire for Dr Ambedkar to be part of Independent India's first Government.[14]

Dr Ambedkar was made a Member of the Drafting Committee of the Indian Constitution (29 August 1947). Later on, he was elected as the Chairman of the Drafting Committee. As the first Union Minister of Law of Independent India and as the Chairman of the Drafting Committee for the proposed Indian Constitution, Dr Ambedkar was now at the pinnacle of his political career. His new responsibilities gave him an indelible and enviable place in laying the foundation of modern India.

* * *

None of these events could have taken place without the support of Mahatma Gandhi. As the Supreme Commander of India's freedom struggle, Mahatma Gandhi was *de facto* in charge—the remote control, some may say.

Set against the backdrop of longstanding conflicts, confrontations and numerous bitter exchange of words between the two prominent figures over the past 17 years, Dr Ambedkar's induction in the Cabinet as well as his placement in the Drafting Committee for the proposed Constitution left everyone stunned, including Dr Ambedkar.

It remains unclear who, if anyone, "swayed" Gandhiji to make such a momentous decision. Going by the scarce research available, neither Jawaharlal Nehru nor Vallabhbhai Patel (whose response was reportedly tepid) seem to have played a decisive role. Evidently, it was a decision made independently by Gandhiji himself.

If this is indeed the case, it would be a truly magnanimous gesture on Gandhiji's part. Dr Ambedkar had previously emphasized

14 Yet another hypothesis is that Muriel Lester, International Organizing Secretary of the Fellowship of Reconciliation and a long-time friend of Gandhiji who hosted him in London during the Second RTC, insisted on Dr Ambedkar's inclusion in the Cabinet.

(on 17 December 1946 in the Constituent Assembly) that "when deciding the destinies of nations, dignities of people, dignities of leaders and dignities of parties ought to count for nothing. The destiny of the country ought to count for everything".

Mahatma Gandhi had actually done it, setting an example for others to emulate, befitting the title of *Mahatma* (a great soul) and, of course, the Father of the Nation.

PART IV

Grand Finale: The Making of the Constitution

CHAPTER FIFTEEN

Constituent Assembly: Dr Ambedkar in Action

On 29 August 1947, the names of the Members of the Drafting Committee were announced. Besides Dr Ambedkar, the Committee included legal luminaries such as Alladi Krishnaswami Ayyar, N. Gopalaswami Ayyangar, K.M. Munshi, Saiyid Mohd. Saadulla, B.L. Mitter and D.P. Khaitan. In the first meeting (29 August 1947), Dr Ambedkar was elected as the Chairman of the Drafting Committee. The Drafting Committee was subsequently reconstituted when N. Madhava Rau was appointed to replace B.L. Mitter, and T.T. Krishnamachari to fill the vacancy created by the death of D.P. Khaitan.[1]

It should be noted, at the outset, that the Constituent Assembly had appointed a number of committees and sub-committees on

---

1 From an excellent Introductory Note contributed by Research and Library Service, Rajya Sabha Secretariat, to the book titled: *Dr B. R. Ambedkar, The Man and His Message: A Commemorative Volume*, edited by Sudarshan Agarwal, the then Secretary-General, Rajya Sabha (New Delhi : Prentice-Hall of India Pvt. Ltd, 1991). This chapter draws extensively from the "inside" information available in this book.

various dimensions of formulating the Constitution and the Reports submitted by these Committees formed the basis for the Drafting Committee to prepare the Constitution of Independent India. As the Chairman of the Drafting Committee, Dr Ambedkar had an uphill task of incorporating the recommendations of these various Committees into the Draft and producing a coherent and acceptable Draft of the Constitution of India. The Draft not only had to be acceptable to the Members of the Constituent Assembly but also "had to be so evolved as to serve the special and immediate needs of an infant democracy and also to stand the test of time". The Constitution was expected to be a valid document for a long time.[2]

The Constitution of any country is essentially a legal document. But by incorporating the principles of socio-economic justice along with political and civil rights which are of fundamental character, Dr Ambedkar, in fact, sought to make the Indian Constitution an effective instrument of social change.

Dr Ambedkar wanted to formulate a Constitution for India that would help establish a *new social order* based on the principles of liberty, equality and fraternity and thus, would pave the way for social, economic and political justice. During the discussions in the Constituent Assembly or its various Committees, whenever any question arose about the downtrodden strata of the society, Dr Ambedkar's "heart would go out for them and he would try to secure maximum political advantage and protection for them".[3] This was of course, natural for him because he had fought, relentlessly, for the upliftment of these sections of society during his entire public life.

---

2 A recent article has observed that the Constitution of India is 'remarkably durable' when compared with the global experience. See Vishnu Padmanabhan with Poopa Dantewadia, 'The Constitution, in Numbers', *The Mint*, 20 January 2020.

3 Introductory Note, *Dr B.R. Ambedkar: The Man and His Message, op cit*, p. 2.

Dr Ambedkar played the pivotal role in the drafting of the Constitution. As an outstanding Constitutional expert, he performed his role with great adroitness, skill, and finesse.

> Dr Ambedkar was fully conscious of the fact that the Constitution which he was going to draft was to serve a nascent democracy like India where many divergent interests and conflicting opinions prevailed. It was indeed a difficult task to produce a code which could effect reconciliation among these forces. Credit for accomplishing this marvel really goes to Dr Ambedkar who gave us a Constitution which has stood the test of time.[4]

In the Herculean task of framing of the Constitution of India, Dr Ambedkar's association was total—in macro as well as micro sense, and meticulous at all levels, despite his failing health. He took keen interest even in the framing of the Rules of Procedure of the Constituent Assembly which came in handy in conducting its business on sound Parliamentary principles. The President and the other Members of the Constituent Assembly looked to him (Dr Ambedkar) for guidance whenever there was any procedural wrangle or when any Member had posed a difficult Constitutional conundrum which required immediate answer.[5]

A senior official,[6] who was in personal contact with Dr Ambedkar from the time the work of the Drafting Committee began, had to say the following (about the style of Dr Ambedkar): "He was a man of genial temperament who was tolerant of arguments, a good listener, a learned critic, and a synthesizer of different ideas. He was clear in

---

4 *Ibid*, p. 6.

5 *Ibid*, p. 5.

6 S.L. Shakdher, Former Secretary-General, Lok Sabha, in 'Dr B.R. Ambedkar and His Contribution in the Constituent Assembly and Parliament', in the book *Dr B.R. Ambedkar: The Man and His Message, op cit*, p. 59.

his thinking and speech and was adept in legal and technical terms. He was also precise and concise in drafting."

Yet another colleague, who as a staff member of the Constituent Assembly had the privilege to be closely associated with Dr Ambedkar's work throughout, said:[7]

> At the meetings of the Drafting Committee, Dr Ambedkar was a picture of confidence. He would not proceed from one clause to another unless all the aspects of the principles embodied in that clause were fully discussed. He would send for the latest books by well-known authorities to post himself with the latest trends in Constitutional development. At the close of each day's meeting of the Committee, he would do a neat summing-up, and this enabled the draftsman to prepare a revised draft, where necessary, for discussion and approval at the next meeting.

* * *

The First Draft of the Constitution was introduced by Dr Ambedkar for the consideration of the Constituent Assembly on 4 November 1948. During the debates in the Assembly, Dr Ambedkar participated extensively elaborating on the draft provisions and amendments moved by the Members. He would patiently answer each and every question raised.

President of the Constituent Assembly, Dr Rajendra Prasad, would often turn to him and say, "Would you like to comment?", "Would you like to throw light on this issue?", or "Dr Ambedkar will now reply". In fact, it would not be wrong to say that *he had the final say in all matters concerning the Constitution during the debates in the Constituent Assembly*[8] [emphasis added].

---

7 P.S. Krishna Mani, Deputy Secretary, Rajya Sabha Secretariat, in 'Dr B.R. Ambedkar: His Role in the Constituent Assembly', *Ibid,* p. 62.

8 Introductory Note., Dr B.R. Ambedkar, The Man and His Message, Ibid, p. 5.

As his close colleague reports[9]:

> Dr Ambedkar's presentation of the basic features of the Constitution was masterly ... Every clause, every amendment, and indeed every suggestion for change or modification received his personal and most careful scrutiny. He would meticulously note down each point made by the Members in the course of the debates in the (Constituent) Assembly, and in his reply would make sure that he had dealt with all those points. ... his ability to marshal facts was remarkable. He was unruffled all the time, would buttress a point by quoting a well-known authority, and, where necessary, also introduce a sense of humour.

At times, some Members of the Constituent Assembly would criticize the provisions in the Draft Constitution and move amendments. If Dr Ambedkar was convinced, he would accept those amendments. At times, he would himself move some amendments to the Draft. If he was not in favour of a particular amendment, he would explain the philosophy behind the provisions, explain why the suggested amendment was not acceptable and then, proceed further.

At this stage, it would perhaps be instructive to re-look at the salient features of the Constitution of India and examine the specific role played by Dr Ambedkar in fine tuning it to perfection.

The Preamble

The Preamble of the Indian Constitution was initially based on the Objectives Resolution adopted by the Constituent Assembly in January 1947. While giving it the final shape, the Drafting Committee made two important changes which made the Preamble more meaningful and reflective of the aspirations of the people.

---

9 P.S. Krishna Mani, *op cit*, p. 64.

First, the Committee replaced the word "independent" by the word "democratic".

The notion of independence is usually subsumed under the word "sovereign". As such, the Drafting Committee felt that there was no need to add the word "independent".

Secondly, the Committee added a new clause. "The Committee also felt it necessary to embody in the Preamble the need for promoting fraternal unity and goodwill among the people in order to ensure the fruits of liberty and equality to all".[10]

Fundamental Rights

According to Dr Ambedkar, the Fundamental Rights were essential for development of the individual and his/her personality and, therefore, they were of paramount importance. Dr Ambedkar firmly believed that the Fundamental Rights were of immense importance also for ensuring social justice. With a view to making the Fundamental Rights operationally meaningful and effective, he felt that it was imperative to make sure that every citizen was in a position to claim those rights and that they were binding on every authority which had been created by law.

As a matter of fact, the draft design of the Fundamental Rights guaranteed in the Constitution was prepared by the Advisory Committee on Fundamental Rights. A number of memoranda were submitted to this Committee by eminent Members like K.M. Munshi, K.T. Shah and others. The Fundamental Rights, as finally adopted by the Constituent Assembly, however, were far more proximate to the suggestions made by Dr Ambedkar than the suggestions by any other Member of the Assembly[11].

---

10 D.C. Ahir, 'Dr Ambedkar: The Chief Architect of the Indian Constitution' in *Dr B. R. Ambedkar, The Man and His Message,* p. 116.

11 Ibid, p. 117.

A close look at Article II, Section I of Dr Ambedkar's own Memorandum[12] and the Constitution of India reveals that, of the 19 Articles dealing with the Fundamental Rights, as many as 15 Articles can be traced to the suggestions put forward by Dr Ambedkar.[13]

Apparently, the remaining four Articles which had not found place in Dr Ambedkar's Memorandum relate to: Abolition of Titles (Article 18); Cultural and Educational Rights of Minorities (Articles 29 and 30); and Right to Property (Article 31).

In the course of discussions on the Fundamental Rights in the Constituent Assembly, several amendments were moved. Interestingly, an amendment moved by H.V. Kamath proposed that a new sub-clause be inserted in order "to guarantee the right to keep and bear arms subject to restrictions imposed by law in the interests of public order, peace and tranquillity".[14]

Responding to the debate, Dr Ambedkar said that it would indiscriminately give the right to every citizen including the ... habitual criminals, to possess arms. In a lighter vein but with a firm patriotic fervour in his tone, Dr Ambedkar added that it should not be forgotten that after Independence the circumstances had changed completely and that in Independent India, what should be insisted upon is *not the right of an individual to bear arms but his duty to bear arms when the stability and security of the State were endangered*[15] [emphasis added].

Dr Ambedkar clarified that the Fundamental Rights cannot be absolute in nature. All rights, he maintained, should necessarily be

---

12 'States and Minorities' discussed in Chapter 14.

13 Ahir, *op cit*, p. 118.

14 In fact, the *Swaraj* Bill of 1895 supposedly inspired by Lokmanya Tilak, had also proposed the same provision (Article 15). See Chapter 9.

15 Ahir, *op cit*, p. 121.

accompanied by corresponding duties. As such, certain reasonable restrictions need to be imposed on these rights in the interest of the State, which ultimately serves the interests of the individuals.

Explaining this concept in the Constituent Assembly, Dr Ambedkar said:

> ... in certain cases those rights must be subject to a certain amount of limitation. Normal, peaceful times are quite different from times of emergency. In times of emergency the life of the State itself is in jeopardy and if the State is not able to protect itself in times of emergency, the individual himself will be found to have lost his very existence.[16]

The Fundamental Rights enshrined in the Constitution of India have been made justiciable. According to the Article 32(2), "the Supreme Court shall have power to issue directions or orders or writs, including writs in the shape of *habeas corpus,* ... whichever may be appropriate, for the enforcement of any of the rights 'conferred' ...".

The provision of this Constitutional remedy emanates almost literally from the provision suggested by Dr Ambedkar in Clause (1) of Section II, Article II of his Memorandum 'States and Minorities'. This is the most effective guarantee for enforcing the Fundamental Rights. In the absence of this provision, the incorporation of the Fundamental Rights in the Constitution would have been meaningless. As Dr Ambedkar emphasized, time and again, rights were real only if they were accompanied by remedies.

Dr Ambedkar in fact, described the importance of this provision (Article 32) in the Constituent Assembly as follows:[17]

---

16 Constituent Assembly Debates (CAD), 9 December 1948, p. 950.

17 Ibid, p. 953.

> If I was asked to name any particular Article in this Constitution as the most important—an Article without which this Constitution would be a nullity—I could not refer to any other Article except this one. It is the very soul of the Constitution and the very heart of it and I am glad that the House has realized its importance.

Untouchability and Social Justice

In a landmark event in the Indian history, on 29 November 1948, the Draft Article 11, which abolished the most abominable practice of Untouchability, was adopted by the Constituent Assembly. Dr Ambedkar had maintained that the problem of Untouchability was of such significance and magnitude that it would be unwise to leave it to be addressed by the Parliament or the State Legislature by enacting separate laws and, therefore, abolition of Untouchability was made a part of the Fundamental Rights.[18]

Dr Ambedkar put in great efforts so as to incorporate into the Constitution specific provisions that would help establish a *new social order*. He firmly believed that some notion of equality should be incorporated into the Fundamental Rights. Therefore, under Draft Article 10, a provision was made that the State could make special provisions for the advancement of any socially and educationally backward classes of citizens or for the Scheduled Castes and Scheduled Tribes.

During the discussion on this Article in the Constituent Assembly, Dr Ambedkar had to reconcile certain conflicting views. While there was a broad consensus about the equality of opportunity for all, the dispute really boiled down to the issue: whether or not, there

18 The Introductory Note, *Dr B.R. Ambedkar: The Man and His Message*, p. 7.

should be reservation for some communities which had remained neglected earlier.

While Dr Ambedkar deftly veered the discussion in favour of reservation, he "was clear in his mind that the concept of equality which is the very basis of democracy should not be compromised or violated".[19]

On a rather tricky question regarding identification of the backward communities, Dr Ambedkar explained that the backwardness of a community could be determined by each local Government. T.T. Krishnamachari, a Member of the Drafting Committee, had asked Dr Ambedkar whether the rule determining the backwardness of a community would be justiciable. While Dr Ambedkar did not give any categorical answer to the question, he expressed his personal view, that it could be a justiciable matter. If the local Government included excessively large number of reserved seats, Dr Ambedkar argued, one could approach the Judiciary and argue that the reservation was of such a magnitude that the rule regarding equality of opportunity had been destroyed and the Court would then decide whether the local Government or the State Government had acted in a reasonable or prudent manner.[20]

Directive Principles of State Policy

After the Fundamental Rights, what immediately follows in the Constitution is the Directive Principles of State Policy, which deal with the concept of socio-economic justice. The Directive Principles, in fact, complement the Fundamental Rights. They aim at directing the State to ensure social and economic justice to individuals. The

---

19 Ibid, p. 7.

20 CAD, 30 November 1948, p. 702.

Directive Principles of State Policy is undoubtedly, a novel and distinctive feature of the Indian Constitution.

Dr Ambedkar defended the inclusion of Directive Principles in the Constitution on the ground that India being a Democratic Republic, it would be the people who would be electing their Government. Whoever came to power would *not* be free to do what they liked because of the very existence of Directive Principles of State Policy. In the exercise of power, the Government would have to respect these Instruments of Instructions. While a Government may not be answerable for the breach of the Directive Principles in a Court of Law, it certainly would have to answer for them before the electorate during the elections.[21]

Uniform Civil Code

Article 44 of the Constitution stipulates that the "State shall endeavour to secure for the citizens a Uniform Civil Code throughout the territory of India". When this Article was being discussed in the Constituent Assembly, Dr Ambedkar, while responding to the questions, clarified that the only area where the Civil law had not been able to invade so far was marriage and succession. He, therefore, found nothing wrong in incorporating certain portions of the Hindu law in formulating new Civil Code applicable to all citizens. These provisions, in his view, would be incorporated not because they were contained in the Hindu law but because they were found to be the most suitable.[22]

---

21 Introductory Note, *Dr B.R. Ambedkar: The Man and His Message,* p. 9.

22 CAD, 23 November 1948, p. 550 and Introductory Note, *Dr B.R. Ambedkar: The Man and His Message,* p. 10.

Expressing his concern at the sentiments of the Muslim community in the matter, Dr Ambedkar clarified that the relevant Article "merely proposes that the State shall endeavour to secure a Civil Code for the citizens of the country. It does not say that after the Code is framed, the State shall enforce it upon all citizens merely because they are citizens. It is perfectly possible that ... in the initial stage the application of the Code may be purely voluntary".

When the Draft Article regarding the Uniform Civil Code was under discussion in the Constituent Assembly, Dr Ambedkar once again clarified his position on the question of personal law. He said:

> I personally do not understand why religion should be given this vast expansive jurisdiction so as to cover the whole of life and to prevent the legislature from encroaching upon that field. After all, what are we having this liberty for? We are having this liberty in order to reform our social system, which is so full of inequities, so full of inequalities, discriminations and other things, which conflict with our Fundamental Rights. It is, therefore, quite impossible for anybody to conceive that the personal law shall be excluded from the jurisdiction of the State.[23]

Dr Ambedkar emphasized that in such matters, the State was only claiming the power to legislate. There was no obligation on the State to do away with personal law. The State was only being given a power. One must not feel that if the State had the power, it would immediately proceed to exercise that power in a manner that might be found to be objectionable by the Muslims or by the Christians or by any community in India. He reminded the Members, particularly those belonging to the Muslim community, that sovereignty was always limited.[24]

---

23 CAD, 2 December 1948, p. 781.

24 Introductory Note, *Dr B.R. Ambedkar: The Man and His Message*, p. 11.

He said: "No Government can exercise its power in such a manner as to provoke the Muslim community to rise in rebellion. I think it would be a mad Government if it did so. But that is a matter which relates to the exercise of the power and not to the power itself."[25]

Constitutional Framework

While speaking about the Constitutional framework, Dr Ambedkar clarified that a modern Constitution could make provision either for Parliamentary system of Government or might opt for a totalitarian or dictatorial form. In India, clearly, we have exercised the choice in favour of Parliamentary democracy.

In order to preserve the democracy in India, Dr Ambedkar emphasized that the "future Government will have to be responsive to the public opinion". Independence was, no doubt, a matter of celebration, but it had thrust upon the Government greater responsibility. After Independence, the Government would not be able to put the blame on the British for its faults. "If things go wrong Government will be responsible for such errors and mistakes."[26]

The Constitution declares India to be a Democratic Republic. A Republic is defined as "a government which derives its powers, directly or indirectly, from the great body of the people and is administered by persons holding their offices during its pleasure for a limited period ... It is essential for such a government that it be derived from the great body of the society, not from a favoured class ...".[27] Such is the democratic form of government that has been

25 CAD, 2 December 1948, p. 782.

26 Introductory Note, Ibid, (both quotes) p. 13.

27 P. Upendra, in *Dr B.R. Ambedkar: The Man and His Message,* p. 81.

provided for in our Constitution. Indeed, Dr Ambedkar has been called the Architect of India's Republican Constitution.[28]

Dr Ambedkar regarded the Constitution as a fundamental document. He was not at all in favour of a liberal procedure for amendment. The Constitution, as a document, defined the position and power of the Executive, the Judiciary and the Legislature. It also defined the limitation of powers of the Executive and of the Legislature as against those of the citizen. Elaborating on this issue, Dr Ambedkar clarified:

> In fact, the purpose of a Constitution is not merely to create the organs of the State but to limit their authority, because if no limitation was imposed upon the authority of the organs, there will be complete tyranny and complete oppression. The Legislature may be free to frame any law; the Executive may be free to take any decision; and the Supreme Court may be free to give any interpretation of the law. It would result in utter chaos.

Dr Ambedkar maintained that the Constitution is a powerful instrument which could improve the well-being of the people. But he was also fully aware of the limitations of the Constitution because there are always minds which operate behind the Constitution … . it is not so much the Constitution but the human element which is more important.[29]

Dr Ambedkar was keen on incorporating into the Constitution all such provisions that would help establish a *new social order* in which no person would be discriminated against on the grounds of "caste, creed, religion, sex and social status". The dexterity of this innovative approach, called for adopting certain progressive

---

28 E.M.S. Namboodripad, in *Dr B.R. Ambedkar: The Man and His Message,* p. 129.

29 CAD, op cit, p. 1662 (17 September 1949).

elements of other Constitutions in such a way that they adequately serve the needs of the resurgent Indian society. That is precisely why, while "incorporating the good elements of the Constitutions of other countries, Dr Ambedkar did not merely copy those provisions and incorporated them into the Constitution but adopted them by making suitable modifications so that they might suit the Indian conditions".[30]

In sum, Dr Ambedkar's contribution to the framing of the Indian Constitution was truly immense—monumental, in fact. No one can deny the claim that he was the *Principal Architect* of the Indian Constitution. He was, in fact, the main guiding force not only behind the Drafting Committee, but for the entire process of formulating, presenting, piloting, explaining and defending the Indian Constitution.

30 Introductory Note, *op cit*, p. 14.

CHAPTER SIXTEEN

Drafting the Constitution of India

Within 15 days after India's Independence, the Constituent Assembly had set up a seven-member Drafting Committee under the Chairmanship of Dr Ambedkar on 29-30 August 1947 to draft a full-fledged Constitution for India.

Dr Ambedkar devoted himself wholeheartedly to the formidable task of drafting the Constitution of India. He worked tirelessly despite his failing health and completed the Draft Constitution of India within six months. The Draft Constitution was submitted to Dr Rajendra Prasad, Chairman, Constituent Assembly, on 14 February 1948, barely a fortnight after the brutal assassination of Mahatma Gandhi.

The Draft Constitution was placed in the public domain for eight months and thereafter, came up for discussion in the Constituent Assembly. Dr Ambedkar introduced the Draft Constitution (315 Articles and 8 Schedules) in the Constituent Assembly on 4 November 1948.

Dr Ambedkar's brilliant exposition of the salient and special features of the Draft Constitution of India can be summarized as under:[1]

---

1 Full address available in Constituent Assembly Debates (Official Report), Vol. VII. Reproduced in BAWS Vol. 13, pp. 49-70. Detailed summary in Jadhav, *Ambedkar Speaks (2013), pp. 464-81.*

Introducing the Draft Constitution, Dr Ambedkar first explained the background process of its preparation. While admitting that the Constitution of "no country could be found to be so bulky", he proceeded to describe the "special features of the Constitution and also meet the criticism that was levelled against it...".

Special Features of the Draft Constitution

1. The Draft Constitution envisaged a Parliamentary System of Government in India which is 'fundamentally different' from the Presidential System of Government prevailing in the United States of America.

   Comparing and contrasting the two systems, Dr Ambedkar underscored the following:

   - Under the US Presidential system, the President is the Head of the Executive, whereas under the Draft Constitution, the President occupies only a ceremonial position. In the case of the latter, the President is the "Head of the State but not of the Executive. He represents the Nation but does not rule the Nation. He is the symbol of the nation".
   - Under the US Constitution, the President has under him a number of Secretaries in charge of different Departments, whereas under the Draft Constitution, the President of India will have under him several Ministers in charge of different wings of administration. However, there is a "fundamental difference". The US President is not bound to accept any advice tendered to him by any of his Secretaries. On the other hand, President of India will be generally bound by the advice of his or her Ministers. The US President can dismiss any Secretary at

any time. The President of the India, on the other hand, has no such power so long as the Council of Ministers commands a majority in Parliament.

- The US Presidential system is based upon the separation of the Executive and the Legislature. As such, the President and his Secretaries are not allowed to be Members of the Congress. "The Draft Constitution does not recognize this doctrine". Not only the Ministers under the Indian Union are Members of Parliament, but only Members of Parliament can become Ministers.
- "Both systems of Government are, of course, democratic and the choice between the two is not very easy". There is a trade-off between "stability" and "responsibility". Broadly speaking, the Presidential form of government tends to be more stable whereas the Parliamentary System is generally more responsible. "The Draft Constitution in recommending Parliamentary system of Executive has preferred more responsibility to more stability".

2. Of the two principal forms of the Constitution—Unitary and Federal—the Draft Constitution opts for a combination of the two–a 'Dual Polity'.

The Draft Constitution is Federal Constitution in the sense that it establishes a Dual Polity, which "will consist of the Union at the Centre and the States at the periphery, each endowed with sovereign powers to be exercised in the field assigned to them respectively by the Constitution".

On the face of it, the 'Dual Polity' of the Draft Constitution somewhat "resembles" the US Constitution. However, the "differences that distinguish them are more fundamental and glaring than the similarities between the two". Essentially, there are two differences: first, in the US there is dual citizenship— Federal as well as States—

whereas the proposed Indian Constitution is based on a single citizenship. "There is only one citizenship for the whole of India. It is Indian Citizenship. There is no State citizenship. Every Indian has the same rights of citizenship no matter in what State he resides".

Secondly, in the US, the Constitutions of the Federal and the State Governments are "loosely connected". This is simply not the case with the proposed Indian Constitution. No State in India has a "right to frame its own Constitution. The Constitution of the Union and of the States is a single frame from which neither can get out and within which they must work".

All Federal Systems, including the American, cannot change their form and become unitary. One of the most distinctive features of the Draft Indian Constitution is that it "can be both Unitary as well as Federal according to the requirements of time and circumstances. In normal times, it is framed to work as a Federal System. But in times of war it is so designed as to make it work as though it was a Unitary System".

Inherent in Federalism are two weaknesses—one is "rigidity" and the other is "legalism". The former arises because a Federal Constitution "cannot but be a written Constitution, and a written Constitution must necessarily be a rigid Constitution". The latter emanates from the fact that a "Federal Constitution means division of Sovereignty" between the Federal Government and the States. "This being the nature of Federalism the Federal Constitution cannot escape the charge of legalism".

In order to contain the problems of "rigidity and legalism, the Draft Constitution follows the Australian plan on a far more extensive scale than has been done in Australia". This includes a "long list of subjects for concurrent powers of legislation, as many as six Articles in the Draft Constitution, where the provisions are of a temporary duration, and which could be replaced by Parliament at any time", and most importantly, "exclusive powers of legislation vested in Parliament" in as many as 91 matters. "In this way the Draft Constitution has secured the greatest possible elasticity in its Federalism ...".

In addition, the Draft Constitution has "added new ways of overcoming the rigidity Draft and legalism ... which are special to it and which are not to be found elsewhere". These include:

a. The power given to Parliament to legislate on exclusively Provincial subjects in normal times, and
b. The provision for facility with which the Constitution could be amended.

It is only in respect of Articles relating to (a) the distribution of legislative powers between the Centre and the State; (b) the representation of the States in Parliament; and (c) the powers of the Courts that the amendment requires ratification by States.

"One can, therefore, safely say that the Indian Federation will not suffer from the faults of rigidity or legalism. Its distinguishing feature is that it is a flexible Federation".

According to Dr Ambedkar, the Draft Constitution has "sought to forge means and methods whereby India will have Federation, and at the same time will have uniformity in all basic matters which are essential to maintain the unity of the country". For this purpose, three mechanisms were proposed:

- A single Judiciary;
- Uniformity in Fundamental laws, Civil and Criminal; and
- A common all-India Civil Service to fill important posts (without depriving the Sates of their right to form their own Civil Service).

Criticism of the Draft Constitution

While introducing the Draft Constitution, Dr Ambedkar responded elaborately to all the criticism. There were 10 points of major criticism and he answered them all, meticulously, as summarized below:

1. The Draft Constitution was criticized on the grounds that there was hardly anything new and that "very little of it can claim originality".

Dr Ambedkar's response was that at that point of time in history of the world, there can hardly be anything new. This is so because the "scope" and "fundamentals" of a Constitution "has long been settled" and "recognized all over the world". For a Constitution "framed so late in the day", the only new things possible are: accommodating "it to the needs of the country" and variations made so as to "remove the faults".

Responding to the charge of "producing a blind copy of the Constitutions of other countries", Dr Ambedkar forcefully added that "the Drafting Committee in performing its duty has not been guilty of such blind and slavish imitation as it is represented to be".

2. The Draft Constitution was severely criticized for reproducing substantially from the Government of India Act, 1935.

Dr Ambedkar's response was two-fold. First, he said: "I make no apologies. There is nothing to be ashamed of in borrowing. It involves no plagiarism. Nobody holds any patent rights in the fundamental ideas of a Constitution." Secondly, he pointed out that what was borrowed related "mostly to the details of administration".

While admitting that administrative details should not have a place in the Constitution, he explained the "necessity" for their inclusion in the Indian case. He referred to Constitutional morality, which is "not a natural sentiment. It has to be cultivated". "We must realize that our people have yet to learn it. Democracy in India is only a top-dressing on an Indian soil, which is essentially undemocratic."

Under the circumstances, the Drafting Committee thought it "wiser not to trust the Legislature to prescribe forms of administration".

3. The Draft Constitution came under criticism because "no part of it represents the ancient Polity of India. … the new Constitution should have been drafted on the ancient Hindu model of a State … raised and built upon Village Panchayats and District Panchayats.' Some people just wanted India to contain so many village Governments …".

Dr Ambedkar responded strongly to this criticism, saying that "these village republics have been the ruination of India". He added, "What is the village but a sink of localism, a den of ignorance, narrowmindedness and communalism? I am glad that the Draft Constitution has discarded the village and adopted the individual as its unit."

4. The Draft Constitution was also criticized for providing special safeguards for minorities.

Dr Ambedkar clarified that "the Drafting Committee has no responsibility. It follows the decisions of the Constituent Assembly". He, however, added: "Speaking for myself, I have no doubt that the Constituent Assembly has done wisely in providing such safeguards for minorities as it has done."

To those who were opposed to minority protection, Dr Ambedkar said two things: (i) "Minorities are an explosive force which, if it erupts, can blow up the whole fabric of the State. The history of Europe bears ample and appalling testimony to this fact; and (ii) The minorities in India have agreed to place their existence in the hands of the majority … . [Minorities] loyally accepted the rule of the majority which is basically a communal majority and not a political majority. It is for the majority to realize its duty not to discriminate against minorities."

5. Some critics of the Draft Constitution argued that the Article "which defines Fundamental Rights is riddled with so many exceptions that the exceptions have eaten up the Rights altogether". Citing the example of the US Constitution, these critics claimed "Fundamental Rights are not Fundamental Rights unless they are also absolute rights".

Dr Ambedkar refuted this criticism pointing out that it is based on "misconception", He argued: "It is incorrect to say that Fundamental Rights are absolute, while non-Fundamental Rights are not absolute. The real distinction between the two is that non-Fundamental Rights are created by agreement between parties while Fundamental Rights are the gift of the law. … it is wrong to say that Fundamental Rights in America are absolute."

According to Dr Ambedkar, the approach adopted by the Draft Constitution is such that instead of formulating Fundamental Rights in absolute terms and then relying on the "Supreme Court to come to the rescue of Parliament … it permits the State directly to impose limitations upon the Fundamental Rights. There is really no difference in the result. What one does directly the other does indirectly. In both cases, the Fundamental Rights are not absolute".

6. The Directive Principles of the State Policy which are a "novel" feature of the Constitution were criticized on the grounds that "they are only pious declarations. They have no binding force".

While admitting that the Directive Principles have no legal force, Dr Ambedkar dubbed the criticism as "superfluous" and said: "I am not prepared to admit that they have no sort of binding force at all. Nor am I prepared to concede that they are useless because they have no binding force in law."

According to Dr Ambedkar, the "Draft Constitution, as framed, only provides a machinery for the government of the country". Directive Principles, he argued, are nothing but the "Instrument of Instructions" to the Legislature and the Executive. It is because of the Directive Principles that

> ... whoever captures power will not be free to do what he likes with it. In the exercise of it, he will have to respect these Instruments of Instructions. He cannot ignore them. He may not have to answer for their breach in a court of law. But he will certainly have to answer for them before the electorate at election time.

7. Some criticized that the Centre was becoming stronger under the Draft Constitution.

In response, Dr Ambedkar argued that "it is difficult to prevent the Centre from becoming strong. Conditions in modern world are such that centralization of powers is inevitable". But he agreed that there was a need to resist "the tendency to make it stronger. It [the Centre] cannot chew more that it can digest. Its strength must be commensurate with its weight. It would be a folly to make it so strong that it may fall by its own weight".

8. The Draft Constitution was condemned for asymmetric Constitutional relations between the Centre and Provinces on the one hand and between the Centre and the Indian [Princely] States, on the other. Under the Draft Constitution, the Princely States were not only "free to create their own Constituent Assembly and to frame their own Constitutions, but were permitted to maintain their own armies".

Dr Ambedkar, in his response, was brutally honest, calling it "very unfortunate" and "quite indefensible". He in fact called it "a most retrograde and harmful provision which may lead to the break-up of the unity of India and the overthrow of the Central Government". He frankly admitted the Drafting Committee was "not at all happy over the matter … . Unfortunately, they could do nothing to improve matters. They were bound by the decisions of the Constituent Assembly and the Constituent Assembly in its turn was bound by the agreement arrived at between the two negotiating Committees".

9. Some critics had objected to the description of India as a Union of States rather than a Federation of States.

Dr Ambedkar clarified that although "India was to be a Federation", it was not being the result of agreement by the States and as such no State had the right to secede. He said, "The Federation is a Union because it is indestructible. Though the country and the people may be divided into different States for convenience of administration the country is one integral whole, its people, a single people living under single '*imperium*' derived from a single source."

He reminded the Constituent Assembly that the US had to wage a "civil war to establish that the States have no right to secession and that their Federation was indestructible".

10. The Draft Constitution came under a "virulent" attack for containing provisions which make amendments difficult.

In response, Dr Ambedkar gave examples of the US and Australian Constitutions, where amendments are really difficult. In comparison, he said, "The provisions for amendment in the Draft Constitution are found to be the simplest."

Some critics had suggested that the Constitution should be amended by simple majority, at least for some years. It was subtly implied that the Constituent Assembly was not elected on adult suffrage and yet, had been given the authority to pass the Constitution by a simple majority. On the other hand, even though the future Parliament would be elected on adult suffrage, it was denied the same authority to amend the Constitution. Critics argued that this was an "absurdity".

In response, Dr Ambedkar argued:

> The Constituent Assembly in making a Constitution has no partisan motive. Beyond securing a good and workable Constitution it has no axe to grind. On the other hand, when the future Parliament meets as a Constituent Assembly, its Members will be acting as partisans seeking to carry amendments to the Constitution to facilitate the passing of Party measures which they have failed to get through Parliament ... Parliament will have an axe to grind while the Constituent Assembly has none.

While concluding his address to the Constituent Assembly, Dr Ambedkar said:

> ... the Constitution as settled by the Drafting Committee is good enough to make in this country to start with.
>
> I feel that it is workable, it is flexible and it is strong enough to hold the country together both in peace time and in war

time. Indeed, if I may say so, if things go wrong under the new Constitution, the reason will not be that we had a bad Constitution. What we will have to say is that Man was vile ... .

* * *

Over the next 13 months or so, the Constituent Assembly went through three readings of the Draft Constitution, discussing and adopting the Articles of the Constitution, one by one.

While replying to the debate during the third (and final) reading of the Constitution on 25 November 1949, Dr Ambedkar made an eloquent and spellbinding speech which is indeed timeless. The Constitution of India was approved the next day, 26 November—which is celebrated now as the 'Constitution Day'.

Dr Ambedkar's Historic Concluding Address

Dr Ambedkar's Concluding Address is arguably the most important speech in his entire public life. Its salient features with some historically important excerpts are presented below[2]:

1. At the outset, Dr Ambedkar explained the details of the timeframe. From the first meeting (on 9 December 1948) the Constituent Assembly worked (until that day, i.e. 25 November 1949) for two years, 11 months and 17 days, during which it held 11 sessions—the first six for discussing the Objectives Resolution and the Reports of various Committees, while the next five sessions were devoted to the consideration of the Draft Constitution. Hundred and fourteen days of the total working days i.e. 165 days, were spent on consideration of the Draft Constitution.

2 Constituent Assembly Debates (Official Report), Vol. X, pp. 972-81. Reproduced in BAWS, Vol. 13, pp. 1206-18.

The Draft Constitution, elected by the Constitutional Assembly on 29 August 1947, held its first meeting the next day and there onwards worked for 141 days on the preparation of the Draft Constitution.

The Draft Constitution, as prepared by the Constitutional Adviser B. N. Rau, "as a text for the Drafting Committee to work upon, consisted of 243 Articles and 13 Schedules", which was expanded by the Drafting Committee to 315 Articles and 8 Schedules, before presenting the first draft to the Constituent Assembly on 4 November 1948.

In its final form, the Draft Constitution contained 395 Articles and 8 Schedules. "The total number of amendments to the Draft Constitution tabled was approximately 7,635. Of them, the total number of amendments actually moved in the House was 2,473".

2. Dr Ambedkar took the trouble of explaining these facts because "it was being said that the Assembly had taken too long a time to finish its work, that it was going on leisurely and wasting public money".

Dr Ambedkar explained that preparation of the Indian Constitution took equal or much lesser time than Canada (29 months) and Australia (111 months). It is true that the Indian Constitution took longer time of preparation that the US (4 months) and South Africa (12 months). However, it must be noted that it is the longest one with 395 Articles as opposed to only seven sections in the US Constitution and 153 sections in the South African Constitution. Moreover, "the makers of the Constitutions of America, Canada, Australia and South Africa did not have to face the problem of amendments. They were passed as moved. On the other hand, this Constituent Assembly had to deal with as many as 2,473 amendments". It is clear, therefore, argued Dr Ambedkar, that "this Assembly may well congratulate itself for having accomplished so formidable a task in so short a time ...".

3. Dr Ambedkar examined the criticism levelled against the Constitution and defended it at length, giving appropriate quotes from the global Constitutional expertise, as he had done earlier while defending the first draft of the Constitution.

In response to a "serious complaint" made on the ground that there is "too much of centralization and that the States have been reduced to Municipalities ...", Dr Ambedkar said:

> The basic principle of Federalism is that the Legislative and Executive authority is partitioned between the Centre and the States not by any law to be made by the Centre but by the Constitution itself. This is what Constitution does. The States under our Constitution are in no way dependent upon the Centre for their legislative or executive authority. The Centre and the States are co-equal in this matter. It is difficult to see how such a Constitution can be called centralism.

Dr Ambedkar admitted the charge that the Central Government has been given the power to override the States. However, he explained that "these overriding powers do not form the normal feature of the Constitution. Their use and operation are expressly confined to emergencies only ...". He also provided the justification below:

> There can be no doubt that in the opinion of the vast majority of the people, the residual loyalty of the citizen in an emergency must be to the Centre and not to the

Constituent States. For, it is only the Centre which can work for a common end and for the general interests of the country as a whole.

4. Reflecting About the Future

Now that India was an independent country, thinking aloud, Dr Ambedkar indicated several of his deep rooted anxieties. "It is not that India was never an independent country. The point is that she once lost the independence she had. Will she lose it a second time? It is this thought which makes me most anxious for the future."

(a) Once upon a time, India was an independent country. But she lost the independence. "What perturbs me greatly is the fact that not only India has once before lost her independence, but she lost it by the infidelity and treachery of some of her own people." "... Will history repeat itself? It is the thought which fills me with anxiety."

(b) Besides our enemies in the form of Castes and Creeds, we are going to have many political parties with diverse and opposing Political Creeds. Will Indians place the country above their Creed or will they place Creed above country? I do not know. But this much is certain that if the Parties place Creed above country, our Independence will be put in jeopardy a second time and probably be lost forever. This eventuality we must all resolutely guard against. We must be determined to defend our Independence with the last drop of our blood.

(c) On January 26, 1950, India would become a Republic, i.e. she would "have a government of the people, by the people and for the people ... What would happen to her democratic Constitution? Will she be able to maintain it or will she lose it again. This is the second thought that comes to my mind and makes me as anxious as the first".

Dr Ambedkar reminded the Assembly:

> There was a time when India was studded with republics, and even where there were monarchies, they were either elected or limited. They were never absolute. It is not that India did not know Parliaments or Parliamentary Procedure ... Buddhist Bhikshu *Sanghas* ... were nothing but Parliaments—[they] knew and observed all the rules of Parliamentary Procedure known to modern times … . This democratic system India lost.

(d) Dr Ambedkar wondered whether India would lose her democracy a second time. He said:

> It is quite possible in a country like India—where democracy from its long disuse must be regarded as something quite new—there is danger of democracy giving place to dictatorship. It is quite possible for this new-born democracy to retain its form but give place to dictatorship in fact. If there is a landslide, the danger of the second possibility becoming actuality is much greater.

(e) Dr Ambedkar asked what we must do if "we wish to maintain democracy not merely in form, but also in fact?" In his considered view,

> The *first thing* in my judgement we must do is to hold fast to Constitutional methods of achieving our social and economic objectives. It means we must abandon the bloody methods of revolution … the method of civil disobedience,

> non-cooperation and *Satyagraha* ... Since the 'Constitutional methods are open, there can be no justification for these unconstitutional methods. These methods are nothing but the Grammar of Anarchy and the sooner they are abandoned, the better for us.

(f) The *second thing* that the people must do is "not to lay their liberties at the feet of even a great man, or to trust him with powers which enable him to subvert their institutions".[3] According to Dr Ambedkar, this precaution is especially important for India because in there,

> *Bhakti* or what may be called the path of devotion or hero-worship, plays a part in its politics unequalled in magnitude by the part it plays in the politics of any other country in the world. *Bhakti* in religion may be a road to the salvation of the soul. But in politics, *Bhakti* or hero-worship is a sure road to degradation and to eventful dictatorship.

(g) According to Dr Ambedkar, the third thing to be done is "not to be content with mere political democracy. We must make our political democracy a social democracy as well. Political democracy cannot last unless there lies at the base of it social democracy". He defined "social democracy" as "a way of life which recognizes liberty, equality and fraternity as the principles of life".

* * *

Dr Ambedkar emphasized that in India, two things are conspicuous by their absence—one is equality and the other

3 Dr Ambedkar quoted philosopher economist John Stuart Mill as well as Irish Patriot Daniel O'Connell.

is "recognition of the principle of fraternity". He said: "On the social plane, we have in India a society based on the principle of graded inequality which means elevation for some and degradation for others. On the economic plane, we have a society in which there are some who have immense wealth as against many who live in abject poverty."

On the 26th of January 1950, we are going to enter into a life of contradictions. In politics we will have equality and in social and economic life we will have inequality. In Politics we will be recognizing the principle of one man one vote and one vote one value. In our social and economic life, we shall, by reason of our social and economic structure, continue to deny the principle of one man one value. How long shall we continue to live this life of contradictions? How long shall we continue to deny equality in our social and economic life? If we continue to deny it for long, we will do so only by putting our political democracy in peril. We must remove this contradiction at the earliest possible moment or else those who suffer from inequality will blow up the structure of political democracy which this Assembly has so laboriously built up. [Accent added]

Dr Ambedkar referred to "fraternity" as "a sense of common brotherhood of all Indians—of Indians being one people. It is the principle which gives unity and solidarity to social life...". Dr Ambedkar opined: "Believing that India 'is a nation is a great delusion'." He asked:

How can people divided into several thousands of Castes be a nation? The sooner we realize that we are not as yet a nation in the social and psychological sense of the word, the better for us. For then only we shall realize the necessity of becoming a nation and seriously think of ways and means of realizing the goal.

* * *

According to Dr Ambedkar, the Castes are "anti-national", firstly because "they bring about separation in social life". And secondly, because they "generate jealousy and antipathy between Caste and Caste ... we must overcome all these difficulties if we wish to become a nation in reality. For fraternity can be a fact only when there is a nation. Without fraternity, equality and liberty will be no deeper than coats of paint".

(h) According to Dr Ambedkar, "... political power in this country has too long been the monopoly of a few ... . This monopoly has not merely deprived them of their chance of betterment, it has sapped them of what may be called the significance of life." He warned that the "urge for self-realization in the down-trodden classes must not be allowed to develop into a Class struggle or Class war". He said: "... the sooner room is made for the realization of their aspiration, the better for the few, the better for the country, the better for the maintenance for its independence and the better for the continuance of its democratic structure. This can only be done by the establishment of equality and fraternity in all spheres of life."

(i) Dr Ambedkar reminded all that "Independence has thrown on us great responsibilities. By Independence, we have lost the excuse of blaming the British for anything going wrong. If hereafter things go wrong, we will have nobody to blame except ourselves. There is great danger of things going wrong. Times are fast changing".

(j) Dr Ambedkar's final advice was:

> If we wish to preserve the Constitution in which we have sought to enshrine the principle of Government of the people, for the people and by the people, let us resolve not to be tardy in the recognition of the evils that lie across our path and which induce people to prefer Government for the people to Government by the people, nor to be weak in our initiative to remove them. That is the only way to serve the country. I know of no better.

* * *

The Constitution: An Assessment

On 6 December 1956 when Dr Ambedkar passed away, Jawaharlal Nehru—the then Prime Minister—delivered a condolence speech in the Lok Sabha where he said:[4] "(Dr Ambedkar) is often spoken as one of the architects of our Constitution. There is no doubt that no one took greater care and trouble over Constitution-making than Dr Ambedkar."

M.L. Dwivedi, one of Dr Ambedkar's colleagues in the Constituent Assembly, wrote: "(Dr Ambedkar) had the onerous responsibility of presenting, piloting and defending the Draft Constitution in the Constituent Assembly. He accomplished this task with remarkable ability and skill.... He was an effective orator and was endowed with such an argumentative skill that he managed always to get his proposals accepted by the Assembly."[5]

---

4 Sudarshan Agarwal (ed), 'Annexure II' in *Dr B.R Ambedkar: The Man and His Message*, p. 208.

5 M.L. Dwivedi, *Dr B.R Ambedkar: The Architect of the Indian Constitution*, pp. 100-01.

On the contrary, in a serious indictment of Dr Ambedkar, Arun Shourie in 1997 labelled him as the "False Manu". Shourie's criticism of Dr Ambedkar rests on three points: First, since the Drafting Committee was responsible only for shaping the Articles drafted by the specialized Sub-Committees, whose suggestions were later discussed in the Plenary Sessions, Dr Ambedkar could not have been in any position to influence the text of the Constitution; secondly, Dr Ambedkar was not privy to the guidelines for each Article, which were decided by the Congress Party. Thirdly, Dr Ambedkar found himself in a minority on numerous occasions in the Sub-Committees, the Drafting Committee and during the Plenary Sessions.

Shourie's criticism of Dr Ambedkar is blatantly false, besides being grossly unfair. In addition to being the Chairman of the Drafting Committee, Dr Ambedkar was a Member of two Committees—the Advisory Committee and the Powers of the Union Committee. In the former case, he was in fact a Member of two important Sub-Committees i.e., the one on Fundamental Rights and also the one on Rights of the Minorities. Moreover, even where Dr Ambedkar was not responsible for drafting the primary texts (i.e. preparing the first drafts), as the Chairman of the Drafting Committee, he was responsible for reformulating them in the form of Articles for the consideration of the Constituent Assembly.

Most importantly, the Constituent Assembly discussed several drafts (there were three readings of the Draft), and each time, unmistakably, it was Dr Ambedkar who, as the Chairman of the Drafting Committee, took the lead in directing the discussion and firming up the formulations. It was Dr Ambedkar who received all the proposals of the various Committees, and therefore, it was his responsibility to reformulate these Articles. Even those editorial tasks were thrust on Dr Ambedkar because of chronic absenteeism of Members of the Drafting Committee.

As one of the Members of the Drafting Committee, T.T. Krishnamachari (who subsequently became the Finance Minister of India) admitted:

> The House is perhaps aware that of the seven members nominated by you, one had resigned from the House and was replaced. One died and was not replaced. One was away in America and his place was not filled up and another person was engaged in State affairs, and there was a void to that extent. One or two people were far away from Delhi and perhaps reasons of health did not permit them to attend. So it happened ultimately that the burden of drafting this Constitution fell on Dr Ambedkar and I have no doubt that we are grateful to him for having achieved this task in a manner which is undoubtedly commendable.'[6]

Even the President of the Assembly, Dr Rajendra Prasad, was full of praise of Dr Ambedkar's contribution as the Chairman of the Drafting Committee, when he observed:

> Sitting in the Chair and watching the proceedings from day to day, I have realised as nobody else could have, with what zeal and devotion the members of the Drafting Committee and especially its Chairman, Dr Ambedkar in spite of his indifferent health, have worked. We could never make a decision which was or could be ever so right as when we put him on the Drafting Committee, and made him its Chairman. He has not only justified his selection but has added lustre to the work which he has done ...[7]

6 CAD, 5 November 1948, p. 231.

7 CAD, 26 November 1949, p. 994.

Therefore, it is abundantly clear that Shourie's criticism is baseless, stemming from what can only be described as "extraneous" reasons. There is not an iota of doubt that Dr Ambedkar played a decisive and determining role in shaping India's Constitution. Not only did Dr Ambedkar redraft the Committee's proposals but also piloted them through the Drafting Committee and the Constituent Assembly to their logical end.

Dr M.V. Pylee, a well-known Constitutional historian and author, says this about Dr Ambedkar's contribution to the framing of our Constitution:[8] "In the Constituent Assembly none else was so forceful and persuasive in arguments, clear and lucid in expression, quick and arresting in debate. And yet, he had always the generosity to concede the credit to a critic who made a valid point and to frankly acknowledge it. Ambedkar's contribution to the Constitution is undoubtedly of the highest order ..."

One of Dr Ambedkar's colleagues, who was closely associated with him during the drafting stage of the Constitution, said:[9]

> Speaking in the Assembly in the closing stages of its deliberations extending three years, Dr B. Pattabhi Sitaramayya, the veteran Congress historian, referred to the 'steam-roller intellect' that Dr Ambedkar brought to bear upon 'this magnificent and tremendous task (of framing the Constitution): irresistible, indomitable, unconquerable, levelling down tall palms and short poppies, whatever he felt to be right he stood by 'regardless of consequences'.

---

8 S.L. Shakdher, 'Dr B.R. Ambedkar and His Contribution in the Constituent Assembly and Parliament' in *Dr B R. Ambedkar, The Man and His Message*, p.56.

9 P.N. Krishna Mani, *Dr Babasaheb Ambedkar, The Man and His Message*, p. 61.

Indeed, the most balanced view about Dr Ambedkar's contribution came from Michael Brecher (Jawaharlal Nehru's biographer), who described Dr Ambedkar as the Chief Architect of the Indian Constitution and as the Field General of the campaign for a new Constitution.

* * *

What has been the impact of the Indian Constitution? An article on 20 January 2020 throws some very interesting light with a global perspective.[10]

The article makes three important observations:

1. The Constitution of India is remarkably durable, especially when compared with the global experience of national Constitutions. A study[11] shows that, "on an average, Constitutions have lasted only 17 years since 1789 (as opposed to 74 years so far of the Indian Constitution)". Constitutions of the post-Colonial countries which gained independence after World War II have been particularly fragile. Illustratively, even before 2009, Pakistan has had three different Constitutions and larger periods of rule without any Constitution. According to this study, out of the 12 Asian countries gaining independence after the World War II, only three Constitutions have survived—those of Taiwan, South Korea and India.

---

10 Vishnu Padmanabhan and Pooja Dantewadia, 'The Indian Constitution, in numbers', *The Mint*, 20 January 2020. https://www.livemint.com/news/india/the-indian-constitution-in-numbers-11579444816636.html

11 Zachary Elkins, Tom Ginsburg and James Melton, *The Endurance of National Constitutions* (New York: Cambridge University Press, 2009).

2. The longevity or endurance of the Indian Constitution is attributed to "its design and the care with which it was drafted ... an elected Constituent Assembly of nearly 300 members spent (nearly) four years debating and defining every aspect of the Constitution – from the idea of India itself to the finer intricacies of federalism. The final product reflected these lengthy deliberations".
3. One of the basic purposes of any Constitution is the rights it endows upon its citizens. As per the data provided by 'Comparative Constitutions Project' (CCP)—an international non-profit data base on global Constitutions, whereas the US Constitution grants 35 rights, the Indian Constitution grants 44 rights. Some of these Constitutional rights, such as Right to Education, are recent additions (for example, RTE become operational in India in 2010) emanating from Constitutional amendments. "This flexibility in amending the Constitution is (also) considered to be one of the biggest factors for the Indian Constitution's endurance."

No one can sum it up better than what was done by one of Dr Ambedkar's associate (P.N. Krishna Mani) mentioned above: "To write about Dr B.R. Ambedkar's role in the Constituent Assembly is to write about the history of the evolution of free India's Constitution."

Does one need to say anything more?

CHAPTER 17

Defending India's Democratic Republic

E.M.S. Namboodiripad, the first Chief Minister of Kerala and long-time General Secretary of the Communist Party of India (Marxist), referred to Dr Ambedkar's contribution to the making of the Indian Constitution as "monumental work" and hailed him as the "Architect of India's Republican Constitution".[1]

As the Principal Architect of India's Constitution, and in his capacity as the (First) Law Minister of India, Dr Ambedkar always advocated for strict adherence to the Constitutional principles, both within and outside the Central Legislative Assembly.

Illustratively, in a speech delivered in Kerala[2] within six months after India became a Republic, Dr Ambedkar emphasized that 'for public conscience to behave in accordance with the Constitutional

1 EMS, 'Dr B.R. Ambedkar: The Architect of India's Republican Constitution' in *Dr B. R. Ambedkar: The Man and His Message,* pp. 129-30.

2 Speech in the Legislative Chamber, Trivandrum, Kerala (10 June 1950). Reported in *Janata* newspaper, 17 June 1950. Reproduced in BAWS Vol. 18(3), pp 218-19.

Provisions is more important than the Constitution itself". He stressed the necessity for both the Constituents i.e. the Government and the people to uphold the "principles and directives as stipulated in the Constitution if the Parliamentary Democracy is to succeed in this country".

Dr Ambedkar also underlined the importance of providing "adequate opportunity" for minority sections of society to "express their opinion and aspiration", which he described as the "basic pillar of Parliamentary Democracy".

Furthermore, Dr Ambedkar underscored the significance of "governance without discrimination" and urged the public to ensure that the "orthodox tendencies of meanness, Untouchability and Casteism do not revive in the country". He also cautioned against the establishment of dictatorship or mobocracy in the country.

Despite reported attempts by the Congress Party to co-opt him, Dr Ambedkar chose to remain free from any political affiliation. He strategically cultivated a distinct identity and built his political support base among the Scheduled Castes. This approach led to increasing discomfort between him and the Congress Party over time. This culmination marked a significant crisis in their relationship—indeed, a head-on collision that surfaced during the controversy surrounding the Hindu Code Bill.

Controversy over the Hindu Code Bill

In 1948, the then Prime Minister Jawaharlal Nehru tasked a Sub-Committee of the Constituent Assembly, chaired by Dr Ambedkar, with drafting the new Hindu Code.

The Hindu Code Bill, which was intended to be an unprecedented comprehensive social reform championed by Dr Ambedkar in the Parliament, became the most contentious issue between him and the Congress leadership.

The purpose of the Bill was to codify the rules of Hindu Personal Law, which were dispersed in various High Court decisions and the Privy Council, resulting in widespread litigation. The Bill essentially sought to codify laws pertaining to seven key aspects: (i) property rights of deceased Hindus; (ii) order of succession among heirs to property; (iii) maintenance; (iv) marriage; (v) divorce; (vi) minority and guardianship; and (vii) adoption.

In sum, the Hindu Code Bill represented a profound social reform in several respects: First, abolition of birthright and not to take property by survivorship; second, equal inheritance rights for daughters; third, conversion of women's limited estate into absolute estate; fourth, abolition of Caste restrictions in marriage and adoption; fifth, the principle of monogamy; and sixth, introduction of provisions for divorce.

Dr Ambedkar presented his version of the Hindu Code Bill to the Constituent Assembly in October 1948. The Bill sparked widespread and bitter controversy as it questioned customs governing the private lives of Hindus, leading to a significant hue and cry. Critics, particularly orthodox Hindus, vehemently opposed the Bill, claiming it a "threat to the sacred nature of Hindu marriage". They argued that marriage and family were fundamental pillars of Hindu society, and that dissolving a marriage would destabilize a tradition that had survived for millennia.

The debate went on for three years. Initially, Prime Minister Nehru had put his full weight behind the Hindu Code Bill, even threatening to resign if it was not passed by Parliament. Despite his initial backing, Nehru never issued a whip and was evidently ineffectual and reluctant to get the conservative Congress members to fall into line. Ultimately, the Hindu Code Bill failed to pass.

There is speculation that Nehru was concerned that Congress MPs would reject the Bill *en masse* and/or that President Dr Rajendra

Prasad, who was decidedly against the Bill, would follow through on his ultimatum not to promulgate it as a law.[3]

Dismayed and repulsed by the withdrawal of the Hindu Code Bill, Dr Ambedkar resigned from the Union Cabinet on 27 September 1951. His resignation over the Bill, which aimed at gender equality among other reforms, holds profound significance. The defeat of the Bill, perhaps, made Dr Ambedkar realize that while the Congress Party endorsed the Constitutional framework of Parliamentary Democracy, many of its members were not prepared to implement concrete reforms that challenged the *status quo* of the society. Clearly, he must have realized that the economic radicalism shown by the emergence of a State-directed and substantially State-owned economy was not matched by corresponding social radicalism, as yet.

No wonder, the statement issued by Dr Ambedkar, after his resignation, concluded:

> The Hindu Code Bill was the greatest social reform measure ever undertaken by the Legislature in this country. No law in the past or the future can be compared to it in its significance. To leave inequality between Class and Class, between sex and sex, which is the soul of Hindu society untouched, and to go on passing legislation relating to economic problems is to make a farce of our Constitution and to build a palace on a dung heap.[4]

True to his Republican spirit, Dr Ambedkar resigned from the Union Cabinet over the issue of gender equality, which he had sought to achieve through the Hindu Code Bill. Nevertheless, hardly

---

3 Jaffrelot, Christophe, *op cit,* p.117.

4 As explained by Gail Omvedt (2004), the term “Class” in this context refers to Caste. During that period, these two concepts were often used interchangeably.

anybody in India gives him credit as a proponent of gender equality; he was merely a Leader of Untouchables, after all.

* * *

At the time of his resignation from the Union Cabinet, Dr Ambedkar's health had significantly deteriorated. He suffered from diabetes, rheumatism, high blood pressure, and chronic leg pain. But an indomitable Dr Ambedkar returned to Opposition politics and immediately began preparing for the first General Elections in the Indian Republic, scheduled for January 1952.

The election manifesto of the Scheduled Caste Federation (SCF) marked a significant departure from the "State socialism" he had previously advocated, shifting towards democratic Republicanism. Dr Ambedkar viewed economic policy on the basis of no 'ism'—only rationalism and pragmatism. According to some experts, this shift represented "a clear retreat from his earlier argument for an economic pattern of State socialism".[5]

Dr Ambedkar's commitment to democratic Republicanism was evident in two key aspects: first, his staunch support for the Parliamentary form of government, which he believed was "the best form of government, both in the interest of the public and in the interest of the individual"; and second, his inclusive strategy that encompassed both "Caste" identity (expanding from Scheduled Castes to Scheduled Tribes and OBCs) and "Class" identity (appealing to "labouring classes").

* * *

The first-ever Parliamentary elections in January 1952 brought disappointment for Dr Ambedkar. The SCF performed miserably,

5 Omvedt, Gail, *op cit*, p.138.

securing only 2.3 per cent of the valid votes and just two seats in the Lok Sabha (one in Bombay Presidency and one in Hyderabad).

Dr Ambedkar himself contested from Bombay City North but lost to Congress candidate Narayan Kajrolkar by a margin of over 14,000 votes. Despite this setback, Dr Ambedkar remained determined to return to Parliament. He requested his trusted colleagues to explore opportunities with various political parties for his nomination to the Rajya Sabha. Eventually, things were "arranged"[6] and Dr Ambedkar was elected as a Member of the Rajya Sabha in March 1952.

As Dr Ambedkar moved towards shaping a broader political identity, there was a need to reformulate his political party as well. Interestingly but not unexpectedly, Dr Ambedkar chose a name for his new party that resonated deeply with him—the Republican Party, drawing inspiration from the party of Abraham Lincoln, which symbolized the emancipation of slaves in the United States.

Dr Ambedkar envisioned the Republican Party of India (RPI) with a comprehensive social democratic agenda aimed squarely against caste-based exploitation. The RPI's mission was explicitly aligned with the interests of all oppressed sections of society. Although formally established after Dr Ambedkar's *nirvana* in 1956, the RPI was founded on the blueprint he had outlined during his lifetime.

* * *

Defending the Republic in the Parliament

As a Member of Parliament in the Rajya Sabha, Dr Ambedkar consistently offered constructive criticism and sage advice on a

6 Keer, Dhananjay, *op. cit*, p. 441. It is not clear what those "arrangements" were; was the Congress' support involved? Most likely, but it is not explicitly clear from the available records.

wide range of issues, always defending the Constitution and India's newborn Republic. Here are some examples:

1. On Constitutional Amendments

While speaking[7] on the Constitution (Third Amendment) Bill, 1954, Dr Ambedkar castigated the Congress Government for its approach to amending the Constitution, at will, 'even without notifying their intention to the people as such …' He asked: "Is the Constitution not different in any sense from an ordinary law? Is it merely a scrap of paper to be amended at the whim of anybody?"

Dr Ambedkar said he had noticed "the great contempt or the low regard or respect which the Government has for the Constitution". He added, "… nobody has any objection to amending it but certainly you ought to treat the Constitution on a somewhat different footing. … Tell the people what you are intending to do and then you may do it. Otherwise, it might become necessary even to amend Article 368 in a manner so as to prevent this facile invasion of the Constitutional provisions."

* * *

When questioned by a fellow Member of Parliament who referenced his earlier comment about burning the Constitution, Dr Ambedkar responded with a metaphorical explanation:[8] "… the reason is this: We built a temple for a God to come in and reside in, but before the God could be installed, the devil had taken possession of it. What else could we do except to destroy the temple?"

---

7 Speech in Rajya Sabha (15 September 1954). Reproduced in BAWS, Vol. 15, pp. 919-24.

8 Speech in Rajya Sabha (19 March 1955). Reproduced in BAWS, Vol. 15, pp. 944-61.

2. On SC/ST Report

While discussing the 'Report of Commissioner for Scheduled Castes and Tribes for 1953', Dr Ambedkar, among other things, said:[9] ".... I do not think that Untouchability will vanish.... It will take years and years. At the same time, there is no reason why we should not strongly agitate for seeing, whether Untouchability goes or not, that the social, economic, political and Constitutional Rights of the Scheduled Castes are fully protected...."

3. On Untouchability

While participating in the Rajya Sabha discussion on 'Untouchability Offences Bill, 1954', (16 September 1954), Dr Ambedkar pointed out some "grave omissions" and certain defective provisions:[10]

1. The Bill does not contain any "provision for the removal of any bar against the exercise of civil and Constitutional rights ...".
2. The Bill is "intended to give protection with regard to civil and fundamental rights" and, therefore, should have included a strong "positive statement", perhaps on the lines of the 'Civil Rights Bill' in the US. Instead, "the Bill seems to give the appearance of a very minor character, just a *dhobi* not washing the cloth ..., or just a *mithaiwala* not selling *laddus* and things of that sort ...".
3. Yet another omission of a "very grave character is that there is no provision against social boycott", which is "one of the greatest and the heinous means which the village community

---

9 Speech in Rajya Sabha (16 September 1954). Reproduced in BAWS, Vol. 15, pp. 925-43.

10 Ibid.

applies in order to prevent the Scheduled Castes from exercising these rights".

4. Dr Ambedkar insisted that the "offences must not be made compoundable ... If the guilty parties by compounding the offence either by payment of a small sum ... are able to get away they can continue their career of harassment of the Untouchables until the moon and the sun are there and Untouchability would never end ...".
5. The Clause relating punishment is "defective". The maximum "punishment prescribed in the Bill is six months' imprisonment or fine which may extend to Rs 500 or both ... There is no minimum fixed?"

   There ought to have been a minimum punishment below which the Magistrate could not go. [Moreover] the punishment is alternative, imprisonment or fine. The Magistrate may very well inflict the alternative punishment of fine and there might be an offender who might be prepared even to pay the five hundred rupees in order to escape the clutches of the law. "What good can such punishment do?"

4. On Centre-State Relations

While discussing the relationship between the Centre (Congress-ruled) and non-Congress State Governments, Dr Ambedkar severely criticized the "intolerant" attitude of the former towards the latter.[11] Dr Ambedkar admonished the Government for misusing Article 356 of the Constitution. He said that "the people have got a very legitimate ground for suspicion that the Government is manipulating the Articles in the Constitution for the purpose of maintaining their own Party in office in all parts of India ...".

11 Speech in Rajya Sabha (14 September 1953) in *Thus Spoke Ambedkar* (Vol. 1 to 3) by Bhagwan Das (1969-79).

Dr Ambedkar was agitated when he asked:

> ... Why be so dogmatic? Why be so tyrannical and why manipulate the Constitution in this way? You are going to bring the Constitution into complete disrepute if you are going to create the impression that all the provisions in the Constitution which we introduced for the purpose of safety are going to be used for the purpose of Party politics. ...

Dr Ambedkar provided the Government with an independent piece of advice: to use the Constitution for its intended purpose. By doing so, not only would they earn respect for themselves but also foster respect for the democratic way of life, which is currently lacking in this country.

* * *

Defending the Republic in Public Domain

Outside of Parliament, Dr Ambedkar continued to share his deep insights for the successful functioning of the democratic Republic of India. Two particularly significant speeches by Dr Ambedkar are summarized here:

1. What is Parliamentary Democracy[12]

At the outset, Dr Ambedkar defined the meaning of Parliamentary Government. He said: "There is a [classic treatise] by Walter Bagehot,... [which] was later expanded by other authorities on Constitutional Government like Harold Laski ... . [They] put the conception of the Parliamentary Government in one sentence ... .

---

12 Speech before the Students' Parliament, DAV College, Jalandhar, Punjab (October 28, 1951). Reproduced in full in BAWS Vol. 17(3).

Parliamentary Government means Government by discussion and not by fisticuffs … ."

According to Dr Ambedkar, in today's world, there are three main things "inherent" in the Parliamentary System of Government:

- "Parliamentary Government means negation of hereditary rule. No person can claim to be hereditary ruler. Whoever wants to rule must be elected by the people from time to time …".
- "No single individual can presume the authority that he knows everything, that he can make the laws and carry the Government. The laws are to be made by the representatives of the people in the Parliament …".
- "… at a stated period those who want to advise the Head of the State must have the confidence of the people in themselves renewed…".

There are "two pillars" on which the Parliamentary system of Government rests. These are the fulcrums on which the mechanism works. Those two pillars are *(i)* an Opposition and *(ii)* free and fair elections … Opposition is the key to a free political life. No democracy can do without it.

Dr Ambedkar further said: "… free and fair elections are necessary for the transfer of power from one section of the community to the other in a peaceful manner and without any bloodshed … Elections must be completely free and fair. People must be left to themselves to choose those whom they want to send to the Legislatures … ."

* * *

A year later, Dr Ambedkar gave an important address[13] on the theme of the successful working of democracy.

---

13 Address at District Law Library, Pune. Details in BAWS, Vol. 17 (3), pp. 472-96.

2. *Conditions Precedent for Successful Working of Modern Democracy*

Dr Ambedkar, in his opening remarks, made some preliminary observations:

- Democracy is "always changing its form. We speak of democracy, but democracy is not always the same".
- Even "in the same country democracy is not always the same … . Democracy keeps on changing its form …".
- Democracy always "undergoes changes in purposes. … The purpose of modern democracy … to bring about the welfare of the people. That is a distinct change in the purpose of democracy…".
- Democracy has been defined by various people differently.

Dr Ambedkar defined democracy as "*a form and a method of government whereby revolutionary changes in the economic and social life of the people are brought about without bloodshed …*".

Against this backdrop, Dr Ambedkar set out the pre-conditions for the successful working of a democracy:

Condition No. 1

The first condition is that 'there must be no glaring inequalities in the society. There must not be an oppressed Class … [or] a suppressed Class. There must not be a Class which has got all the privileges and a Class which has got all the burdens to carry … such an organization of a society has within itself the germs of a bloody revolution, and perhaps it would be impossible for the democracy to cure them…'.

One of the reasons for breakdown of democracies the world over, he said, is 'the existence of … social cleavages'.

Condition No. 2

The second condition for the successful working of a democracy is 'the existence of an Opposition'. He explained that '... democracy means a veto of power. Democracy is a contradiction of hereditary or autocratic authority. ...at some stage somewhere there must be a veto on the authority of those who are ruling the country, [i.e. elections]'.

According to Dr Ambedkar:

Democracy requires ... not only that the Government should be subject to ..., long-term veto of five years, at the hands of the people, but there must be an immediate veto. There must be people in the Parliament immediately ready there and then to challenge the Government .... democracy means that nobody has any perpetual authority to rule, but that rule is subject to sanction by the people ....

Dr Ambedkar emphasized: "Opposition means that the Government is always on the anvil. The Government must justify every act that it does to those of the people who do not belong to its Party ... there must be someone to show whether the Government is going wrong. And this must be done incessantly and perpetually ... ."

Condition No. 3

The third condition is 'equality in law and administration'. Dr Ambedkar emphasized that 'one need not at this stage dilate too much on equality before the law but rather on equality of treatment in administration'.

Condition No. 4

The fourth condition is the 'observance of Constitutional morality'. Dr Ambedkar explained that a Constitution which

> 'contains legal provisions, [is] only a skeleton.... The flesh of that skeleton is to be found in what we call Constitutional morality. ... people must be ready to observe the rules of the game...'.

Before concluding his thought-provoking address, Dr Ambedkar added three fundamental observations:

- "... in the name of democracy there must be no tyranny of the majority over the minority. The minority must always feel safe that although the majority is carrying on the Government, the minority is not being hurt, or the minority is not being hit below the belt ...".
- "... democracy does require the functioning of moral order in society. Democracy means a free Government ...". Free Government means that in vast aspects of social life people are left free to carry on without interference of law, or if law has to be made, then the lawmaker expects that society will have enough morality in it to make the law a success. Quoting Harold Laski, Dr Ambedkar added: "The moral order is always taken for granted in democracy. If there is no moral order, democracy will go to pieces ... ."
- "... democracy requires 'public conscience'." Dr Ambedkar elaborated: "Public conscience means conscience which becomes agitated at every wrong, no matter who is the sufferer and it means that everybody whether he suffers that particular wrong or not, is prepared to join him in order to get him relieved ... ." He added: "[If] there is no 'public conscience' ... the minority which is suffering from injustice gets no help from others for the purpose of getting rid of this injustice. It ... develops a revolutionary mentality which puts democracy in danger ... ."

Dr Ambedkar wrapped up his address with a warning, which is timeless. He said:

> ... the subject about which I have spoken this evening, ... is a subject of the greatest importance to this nation. We have somehow developed the idea that we have got Independence. The Britishers have gone. We have got a Constitution which provides for democracy. Well, what more do we want?
>
> We cannot rest, as we say, on our ears, and do nothing more. Let me warn you against this kind of smug feeling that with the making of the Constitution our task is done. It is not done. It has only begun ... .
>
> ... I think we ought to be very cautious and very considerate regarding our own future. You ought to consider whether we ought not to take some very positive steps in order to remove some of the stones and the boulders which are lying in our path in order to make our democracy safe ... .

CHAPTER 18

A Summing-Up

The people of India, having solemnly resolved to constitute India into a Sovereign Democratic Republic, on 26 November 1949, adopted, enacted and gave to themselves the Constitution. India became a Sovereign Democratic Republic on 26 January 1950.

India has come a very long way. Over two and half millennia (2,500 years) ago, during the lifetime of Gautam Buddha, India was dotted with Republics. India knew what Democracy was, but lost it somewhere along the way.

India becoming a Republic (and that too, the world's most populous one) was nothing less than an epoch-making event.

This significant milestone in world history, of course, did not unfold overnight. It was the culmination of a long-drawn process of Constitutional Reforms initiated by the then ruling British Government of India as far back as 20 August 1917. On that day, the British Government adopted a policy of "Increasing association of Indians ... with a view to the progressive realization of responsible government in India ...".

This process of Constitutional Reforms, spanning nearly 33 years, inevitably had many ups and downs. Key milestones included the Montagu–Chelmsford Reforms (1918), the Southborough

Committee (1919), the Government of India Act (1919), the Simon Commission (1928), the Round Table Conferences (1931-33), the Lothian Committee (1932), the Government of India Act (1935), the Proposal for Federation of India (which was the British version for the proposed Constitution of India) (1935), the Cripps Mission (1942) and finally, the Cabinet Mission (1946).

Interspersed with these British-led reforms were several Indian efforts to draft a *Swaraj* Constitution. These included efforts by Lokmanya Tilak (1895), Ms Annie Besant (1925), Motilal Nehru (1928) and Tej Bahadur Sapru (1945).

While each of these great Indian leaders contributed to the formulation of the Indian Constitution in their own distinct, yet limited capacities, the only Indian leader who remained unwaveringly dedicated to the Constitutional Reform process at every stage was Dr Babasaheb Ambedkar (Mahatma Gandhi did not participate in the first and third Sessions of the Round Table Conference, while Jawaharlal Nehru abstained from all three Sessions).

It was a remarkable coincidence that the historic announcement in the British Parliament—the Montague (August) Declaration—on 20 August 1917, marking the beginning of Constitutional Reforms for greater Indian participation, was made just *one* day before Dr Ambedkar returned to India (after having to discontinue his advanced education in England). From then onwards, for every significant reform proposal made by the British, starting from the Southborough Committee (1919) to the Cabinet Mission (1946), Dr Ambedkar was actively involved. He meticulously analysed each component, testified before all relevant Missions and Commissions, fully participated in all three Sessions of the Round Table Conference and provided extensive commentary on each proposal for Constitutional Reform.

What is more, Dr Ambedkar thoroughly examined and offered critiques on various *Swaraj* Constitutions. Not knowing that he was going to be chosen as the Chairman of the Drafting Committee for the Constitution of India, Dr Ambedkar even drafted his version of the Indian Constitution in March 1947.

The crowning glory was, of course, when as the Chairman of the Drafting Committee for the Indian Constitution and as the first Law Minister of Independent India, Dr Ambedkar not only gave final shape to the Indian Constitution but also successfully piloted the draft Constitution through three readings in the Constituent Assembly for nearly four years. This is how the edifice of the Constitution of India came alive.

* * *

Traditional wisdom in India is rich with narratives recounting the life and times of Mahatma Gandhi and Jawaharlal Nehru. Pedagogical teachings rightly depict Gandhiji and Nehru as leaders of national stature, celebrated through prose, poetry, skit and song. Regrettably, Dr Ambedkar appears only briefly, if mentioned at all. And when he does make an appearance, he is invariably referred to as the "Leader of Untouchables". Dr Ambedkar's portrayal in educational discourse has always been marginal—as a Caste leader or advocate for the subalterns, but never as a national leader.

Even though Dr Ambedkar's profound contribution in shaping the final version of the Indian Constitution has been well-documented by none other than Dr Rajendra Prasad, who was the Chairman of the Constituent Assembly throughout, some people have tried to cast a shadow on his true role and sow doubt among the Indian populace by undermining Dr Ambedkar's contribution.

Are we, the people of India, so ungrateful? Why was it that his name was only considered for the Bharat Ratna award when there was a non-Congress government at the Centre? Why was the Bharat Ratna denied to Dr Ambedkar for 34 years, only to be awarded posthumously in 1990 by the National Front Government? Why do we not find Dr Ambedkar in the pantheon of great national leaders of India?

Dr Ambedkar was hailed as the "Chief Architect of Indian Constitution" and the "Field General of the campaign for a new Constitution". Regrettably, no Indian leader was gracious enough to acknowledge this fact. Interestingly, these accolades came from Canadian Political Scientist Professor Michael Brecher, who authored a biography of Jawaharlal Nehru.

All said and done, I think the time has come to rectify a historic injustice. We must, finally, recognize Dr Babasaheb Ambedkar for who he truly was—the Man who shaped the Republic of India!

Well, better late than never, but nothing less will do.

References

Andrews, C.F. 1930. *Routledge Revivals: India and the Simon Report*. London: Routledge p. 31. https://doi.org/10.4324/9781315445007.

Agarwal, Sudarshan (ed.). 1991. *Dr B.R. Ambedkar: The Man and His Message*. A Commemorative Volume. Delhi: Prentice-Hall of India.

Ambedkar, Dr Babasaheb. 1979-2012. *Writings and Speeches (BAWS):* Vol. 1-22. Mumbai: Government of Maharashtra.

Anand, S. 2012. 'B.R. Ambedkar Greater than Nehru?' *Outlook,* 12 August 2012.

Austin, Granville. 1966. *The Indian Constitution: Cornerstone of a Nation*. Oxford: Clarendon Press.

Bombay High Court. 1908. 'Emperor *vs* B. G. Tilak.' 22 July. https://indiankanoon.org/doc/1430706/ (accessed on 9 January 2021).

Burke, Edmund. 'Speech on moving his resolutions for Conciliation with the British Colonies.' 22 March 1775. Eighteenth Century Collections Online.

——— 1790. *Reflections on the Revolution in France*. London: James Dodsley.

Centre for Law and Policy Research. 'Nehru Report.' CADIndia. clpr.org.in. (accessed on 7 May 2020).

Chand, Tara. 1972. *History of the Freedom Movement in India*, Vol. III. New Delhi: Publications Division, Ministry of Information and Broadcasting.

Chandra, Bipan. 2009. *History of Modern India*. Hyderabad: Orient Blackswan.

Chandra, Bipan, Mridula Mukherjee, Aditya Mukherjee, et al. 1989. *India's Struggle for Independence 1857-1947*. Delhi: Penguin Books.

Chintamani, C. Yajnesvara (ed.). 1901. *India Social Reform in Four Parts – Being a Collection of Essays, Addresses and Speeches* Part II. Madras: Thompson & Co., Reprint 2007.

Clarke, Blake. 1950. 'Ambedkar: The Untouchable.' *Christian Herald*, March 1950.

Coupland, R. 1944. *The Indian Problem: Report on the Constitutional Problem in India*. New York: Oxford University Press. www. questia. com (accessed on 6 May 2020).

Danzig, Richard. 1968. 'The Announcement of August 20th, 1917.' *The Journal of Asian Studies* Vol. 28, No. 1 (November 1968): pp. 19-37. https://doi.org/10.2307/2942837 (accessed 28 June, 2020).

Das, Bhagwan (ed.). 1969-79. *Thus Spoke Ambedkar* Vol 1-3. Lucknow: Dalit Today Prakashan; New Delhi: Samyak Prakashan.

De, Rohit. 2016. 'Constitutional Antecedents.' In *The Oxford Handbook of the Indian Constitution*, edited by Sujit Choudhary, Madhav Khosla and Pratap Bhanu Mehta. Oxford, UK: Oxford University Press.

Desai, Mahadev. 1953. *The Diary of Mahadev Desai* Vol. 1. Mumbai: Navajivan Publishing House.

Durant, Will. 1926. *The Story of Philosophy*. New York: Simon & Schuster.

Dwivedi, M.L. 1991. 'Dr B.R. Ambedkar: The Architect of the Indian Constitution.' In *Dr B.R. Ambedkar: The Man and His Message*. A Commemorative Volume, edited by Sudarshan Agarwal. New Delhi: Prentice-Hall of India, pp. 100-01.

Elkins, Zachary, Tom Ginsburg and James Melton. 2009. *The Endurance of National Constitutions*. New York: Cambridge University Press.

Gaikwad, S.M. 1998. 'Ambedkar and Indian Nationalism.' *Economic and Political Weekly* Vol. XXXIII, No. 10 (7 March 1998).

Gandhi, M.K. 1940. *An Autobiography: The Story of My Experiments with Truth*. Translated by Mahadev Desai. (New Delhi: General Press).

Gordon, Johnson. 1974. *Provincial Politics and Indian Nationalism:*

Bombay and the Indian National Congress 1880-1915. New York: Cambridge University Press.

Gore, M.S. 1993. *The Social Context of an Ideology: Ambedkar's Political and Social Thought*. New Delhi: Sage Publications.

Government of India. 1931. 'Proceedings of Sub-Committee No. VI (Franchise).' Calcutta: Central Publication Branch.

Guha, Ramachandra. 2016. *Gandhi Before India*. Gurugram: Penguin Random House.

Jadhav, Narendra (ed.). 2013a. *Ambedkar Speaks* Vol 1-3. New Delhi: Konark Publishers.

——— 2013b. *Ambedkar Writes* Vol 1-2. New Delhi: Konark Publishers.

——— 2014. *Ambedkar: Awakening India's Social Conscience*. New Delhi: Konark Publishers.

——— 2015. *Ambedkar: An Economist Extraordinaire*. New Delhi: Konark Publishers.

——— 2016. 'India and the United States: Caste, Race, and Economic Growth.' Sixth Annual Patrick O'Meara International Lecture at Indiana University Bloomington, 14 November.

Jaffrelot, Christophe. 2005. *Dr Ambedkar and Untouchability: Analyzing and Fighting Caste*. New Delhi: Permanent Black.

Joseph, Tony. 2018. *Early Indians: The Story of Our Ancestors and Where We Came From*. New Delhi: Juggernaut Books.

Khabde, D.T. 1985. PhD diss. Dr Babasaheb Ambedkar Marathwada University. https://shodhganga.inflibnet.ac.in

Khairmode, C.B. 1984-2008. *Dr Bhimrao Ramji Ambedkar* Vol. I-XII (Marathi). Pune: Sugava Prakashan.

Keer, Dhananjay. 1954. *Dr Ambedkar: Life and Mission*. Bombay: Popular Prakashan.

Kumar, Aishwarya. 2012. 'The Lies of Manu'. *Outlook*, 20 August 2012. https://magazine.outlookindia.com/story/the-lies-ofmanu/28193.

Lancaster, Lane W. 1959. *Masters of Political Thought: Hegel to Dewey*, Vol. 3. London: George G. Harrap and Co Ltd.

Laski, H. 1925. *A Grammar of Politics*. London: George Allen and Unwin Ltd.

Lelyveld, Joseph, 2011. *Great Soul: Mahatma Gandhi and His Struggle with India*. Delhi: Harper Collins Publishers and the India Today Group.

McCutcheon, Richard. 1989. 'The Impact of the Jallianwala Bagh Massacre on Gandhi'. PhD diss. McMaster University. Available from http://hdl.handle.net/11375/11927

Mehta, M. 2005. 'Gandhi and Ahmedabad, 1915-20.' *Economic and Political Weekly* Vol. 40, No. 4 (22 January 2005).

Menon, V.P. 1957. *The Transfer of Power in India*. Delhi: Orient Longman.

Nwasike, Joan and Dustan Maina (ed.). 2018. *Key Principles of Public Sector Reforms: Commonwealth Case Studies*. London: Commonwealth Secretariat.

Omvedt, Gail. 2004. *Ambedkar: Towards an Enlightened India*. Delhi: Penguin.

Padmanabhan, Vishnu with Poopa Dantewadia. 2020. 'The Constitution, in Numbers.' *The Mint*, 20 January 2020.

Power, P.F. 1969. 'Gandhi in South Africa'. *The Journal of Modern African Studies* Vol. 7, No. 3 (1969).

Prasad, R. 1949. *Satyagraha in Champaran*. Ahmedabad: Navajivan Publishing House.

Pyarelal. 1932. *The Epic Fast*. Ahmedabad: Mohanlal Maganlal Bhatt.

Rajasekhariah, A. M. 1971. *B.R. Ambedkar: The Politics of Emancipation*. Bombay: Sindhu Publications.

Schwartzberg, Joseph E. (ed). 1978. *A Historical Atlas of South Asia*. Chicago: University of Chicago Press. https://dsal.uchicago.edu/reference/schwartzberg/fullscreen.html?object=110. (accessed on 24 May 2020).

Sethi, Pravat Ranjan. 2019. 'Gandhi and the Jallianwala Bagh Massacre and Beyond.' *Mainstream Weekly* Vol. LVII, No. 18 (2019). https://www.mainstreamweekly.net/article8659.html (accessed on 22 July 2020).

Shanker, Rajkumari. 1969. *The Story of Gandhi*. Delhi: Children's Book Trust. https://www.mkgandhi.org/ebks/The%20Story%20of%20Gandhi.pdf

Shraff, Anne. 2008. *Mahatma Gandhi* (20th Century Biographies). California: Saddleback Educational Publishing.

Som, Reba. 1994. 'Jawaharlal Nehru and the Hindu Code.' *Modern Asian Studies* (1994) : pp. 185-87.

Sorokin, Pitirim. 2002. *The Ways and Power of Love*. West Conshohocken, PA: Templeton Press.

Tariq, Abdur-Rahman (ed.). 1973. *Speeches and Statements of Iqbal.* Lahore: Sh. Ghulam Ali.

Tendulkar, D.G. 1951. *Mahatma: Life of Mohandas Karamchand Gandhi.* Bombay: Vithalbhai K. Jhaveri.

The Indian National Congress. 'Indian National Congress – INC Timeline.' https://www.inc.in/en/inc-timeline/1905-1915 (accessed on 28 June 2020).

The Indian National Congress. 1909. Madras: G. A. Natesan.

The Times. 1921. 'New Indian Councils: Failure of Boycott Movement.' No. 42613 (8 January 1921), p. 9.

The Times. 1921. 'New Era For India: Delhi Parliament Opened, King's Messages.' No. 42641 (10 February 1921): p. 10.

Todd, A.M. 2004. *Mohandas Gandhi*. New York: Infobase Publishing.

Vundru, Raja Sekhar. 2012. 'The Other Father.' *Outlook,* 20 August 2012.

Weber, Thomas. 2004. *Gandhi as Disciple and Mentor*. New York: Cambridge University Press.

Index

About the Author

DR NARENDRA JADHAV is a multi-faceted professional, renowned as an Economist, Educationist, Academic, Administrator and Author (in English, Marathi and Hindi). And now, he has also taken on the roles of a web series anchor and producer, and a podcaster.

Until April 2022, Dr Jadhav served as a Member of Parliament in the Rajya Sabha (nominated by the President of India). As an independent MP, Dr Jadhav carved out a distinct place for himself through his studious interventions in the Parliament, establishing new standards of excellence for nominated MPs.

Currently, Dr Jadhav is producing a comprehensive web series on the Indian Constitution, spanning nearly 60 hours and featuring insights from 35 MPs, 20 Judges (Supreme Court and High Court) and other top legal luminaries. He also hosts an audio visual podcast series titled 'Bhim Bhashya', focusing on Dr Ambedkar, on his YouTube channel 'Dr Narendra Jadhav World'.

Dr Jadhav serves as an Independent Director for five corporates, including two from the Tata Group, and Jain Irrigation Systems Ltd. He is also serving as a Member of Governing Council/Advisory Council of several Universities. Over the past seven years, Dr Jadhav has been serving as a Visiting Professor simultaneously at four universities, including Ashoka University.

With a PhD in Economics from Indiana University, USA, Dr Jadhav has had an illustrious career spanning nearly five decades in public service. Some of the distinguished positions held by him include Member – Planning Commission; Member, National Advisory Council (NAC); Vice-Chancellor of Savitribai Phule Pune University; Adviser, International Monetary Fund (IMF), and Chief Economist, Reserve Bank of India (and also for Afghanistan and Ethiopia). Dr Jadhav recently chaired the Advisory Committee on RBI History: Volume V (1977-2007).

Dr Jadhav is a prolific writer. He has authored or edited 44 books: 22 in English, 14 in Marathi and 8 in Hindi, in addition to 32 official reports on various public policy issues and around 200 research papers and articles. His family biography Untouchables (Simon and Schuster, USA) is an international bestseller, translated into 15 languages, including French, Spanish, Korean and Thai, with its Marathi original, *Aamcha Baap Aan Amhi*, achieving unprecedented success with 200 editions and receiving a Sahitya Akademi Award for its Punjabi version.

A celebrated public figure, Dr Jadhav is recipient of 73 national and international awards for his contribution to the fields of Economics, Education, Literature and Social Work, including four Honorary D.Litt. Degrees and the title of the 'Commander of the Order of Academic Palmes' by the Government of France.